DEATHS AT DAVOS 2.0

By Thierry Malleret

For MA,
Without whom this book wouldn't have seen the light of day.
With love and gratitude.

FROM THE SAME AUTHOR

Deaths at Davos
Amazon, 2024 - novel

The Great Narrative (with Klaus Schwab)
Forum Publishing, 2022 - essay

The Great Reset (with Klaus Schwab)
Forum Publishing, 2020 – essay

Dix bonnes raisons d'aller marcher
Paulsen, 2017 – essay

Les riches sont-ils méchants ?
Slatkine, 2013 – novel

Six Global Mega Trends and How to
Make Them Work for You
Versilio, 2013 – essay

Disequilibrium – A World Out of Kilter
Bookbaby, 2012 – essay

Global Risk – Business Success in
Turbulent Times (with Sean Cleary)
Palgrave Macmillan, 2007 - essay

Crimes sans châtiments
Maxima, 2002 – novel

La roulette russe
Le Rocher, 1998, novel

Alerte aux fous de Dieu
Flammarion, 1997 – novel

Le montage caucasien
Le Rocher, 1996 – novel

Conversion of the Defense Industry
in the Former Soviet Union
Institute for East-West security Studies, 1991 - essay

L'armée rouge Face à la perestroïka
Complexe, 1991 – essay

FOREWORD AND ACKOWLEDGEMENTS

"Deaths at Davos 2.0" is the sequel to "Deaths at Davos", published in 2024.

This short geopolitical thriller is a work of fiction. All the characters, businesses, and places, whether named or unnamed, and events, incidents, and dialogues in this story are either the product of the author's imagination or used in a fictitious manner.

I hope it is an easy and exciting read, and a bit more besides. Through fiction and the power of imagination, it aims to shed light on some very real issues of global significance.

I am most grateful to the experts, journalists and policymakers from varied backgrounds who generously contributed their ideas and insights. And to Fabienne Stassen for the velocity of her remarkable editing.

If this novella has aroused your curiosity, any questions or remarks will be read with interest and gratitude at deathsatdavos@gmail.com.

1 – Saturday, 18 January 2025

Sometimes, reality trumps imagination. Sometimes, it even outruns fiction.

Such was the thought doing the rounds of Olena Kostarenko's mind as she sat on the terrace of the Hotel Schatzalp, soaking up the welcome warmth of the winter sun. With more than a soupçon of understatement, the last 12 months hadn't been easy. In the intervening year, since last in Davos, Olena had seen the hopes she'd harboured so fervently evaporate, one by one. Ukraine, her country, was still at war, fatigued and fracturing within while fast falling from the top of the international community's list of priorities. So, too, were the environmental policies to which she'd devoted so much time and energy in recent years. And now, in just two days' time, Donald Trump would take up residence in the White House – mission accomplished for 0047. On offer: new beginnings.

And yet Olena was determinedly looking forward to the next few days, excited and apprehensive in equal measure. Her mission was far from accomplished. On offer: change for the better... or abject failure.

Leaning back on the wicker lounger, Olena stared out at the horizon as she put her well-thumbed copy of *The*

Magic Mountain down on the small side table. In 1913, the idea for the novel had come to Thomas Mann on this very same terrace. He then spent nearly 12 long years working on it until its publication in November 1924. Mann's chef-d'oeuvre was to prove prescient; it read the omens and warned of the dangerous times ahead. The Europe to come of the 1930s would be torn between apathy and despair, grappling with conflicting ideologies in a fragmented and disorderly world. How could it have come to this? Isn't today's world in a similarly dangerous place? pondered Olena. What had Thomas Mann seen from this terrace that others had failed to observe? For a little while, still gazing out at the mountains, her musing continued before she reluctantly concluded that as most looked on incredulous and incrementally unshockable, reality was outstripping the wildest of imaginations – and making little sense as it did so.

With a deep breath of crisp mountain air, Olena bought herself back to the reality of that January 2025 afternoon. Marvelling at the Alpine scenery, her eyes methodically moved from peak to peak. At each summit a question: Might this year's Circle annual meeting achieve something? Might it yield more than the customary huckster talk and empty reassurances? Might it go beyond banality? Might the elites deliver? Who was she kidding? Who was drifting into the realm of fiction now? She swiftly rejected these ideas. As always, like Hans Castorp, *The Magic Mountain*'s central character, the Don, in his own enclosed "sanatorium," the secluded setting of the Congress Centre, would haplessly grapple with the major global issues of the day, torn between and buffeted by other people's opinions. Meanwhile, in the shadows, just like 100 years ago, the global powers' secret agents would be having a field day in the apparently peaceful microcosm of Davos.

This, Olena knew for sure.

She checked her watch. 12.30pm. It was time for her to go. She'd already had two failed attempts to make contact with her "target." She was running out of chances. This afternoon, she had to succeed. Failure was not an option. She walked straight to the station and boarded the funicular, settling in front of the panoramic window. Three hundred metres below, down in Davos, people looked like pawns being moved around by some invisible grand master. Above, in the distance, the majestic peaks of Pischahorn, Jakobshorn, Rinerhorn, with Piz Ela in the background, formed a monumental mineral barrier, swathed in white. Olena had always thought that the mountains had this amazing capacity to put humans in their rightful place – it was a matter of perspective and of proportion. Enlivened by this abundance of space, stunned by the beauty of it all, her spirits rose. The doubts of the past weeks were evaporating. All of a sudden, she felt confident. Yes, it was the challenge of a lifetime, but she'd be up to it.

Olena got out at Davos Platz, turned left and walked to the end of Obere Strasse, where it merges with the Promenade. She then turned in the direction of the Congress Centre, repeatedly looking over her shoulder as she walked. In the surrounding streets, a melee of high-vis-jacketed labourers and khaki-camouflage-clad soldiers were at work erecting fences and preparing to close the city's main artery, all under the watchful eye of the Graubünden police resplendent in navy blue. In a few hours, walking in the security zone of Davos without a badge would be impossible. It was now or never. She was armed with some inside info about the Don's daily movements and just hoped this time she'd got her timings right. Passing the Kirchner Museum, she noticed a compact group of men in black on the other side of the pavement.

Bingo! There he was.

As an integral part of a rigorous, personal wellbeing programme, particularly pertinent in the stressful days running up to the annual meeting, the Don was taking a brisk walk, surrounded by his private security team. In Davos, he never ventured outside without half-a-dozen bodyguards, enough to keep unwelcome visitors at bay. Not that he feared for his life, but rather for his reputation. He'd had more than what he regarded as his fair share of bad experiences with journalists cornering him with questions he'd prefer not to answer. But this was Olena's chance and there wouldn't be another.

'Sir, sir!' she shouted from a slight distance, raising her arm and flashing a broad smile.

He turned his head towards her and stopped, staring at his former employee as she crossed the street towards him. The Don looked at Olena with an expression of disbelief, followed by one of ambivalence, somewhere between irritation and curiosity.

As she approached, three bodyguards stepped in to stop her coming any closer. With a wave of his hand, the Don told them to stand aside.

'It's Olena, Sir. Olena Kostarenko. Do you remember me?'

A rhetorical question. Of course he did! How could he not?

The sound of her voice provoked very uncomfortable memories. His look became a glare.

The last 12 months had taken their toll. She had aged and was noticeably thinner but her innate attractiveness, that had never been wasted on the Don, was not diminished. She was taller than him, slender. The impeccable geometry of her face had a classical beauty, with a proud bearing, making her seem slightly aloof and secretive, which only added to her charm. His eyes met hers: piercingly green, all-seeing yet remote. More irksome memories flooded back: her unfulfilled promise and his misplaced hopes for her as one of the Circle's "aspiring leaders," the bitter disappointment when she'd rejected an offer to work in his private office, her peripheral but problematic involvement in last year's Davos debacle that ended up costing the Circle so much of its reputation. And here she was, back in Davos. *What on earth is she doing here? How dare she?* he muttered to himself.

'Of course I do!' he replied stiffly. 'How are you, Olena?'

'I am well, Sir, but the past 12 months have been tough, to say the least. Ukraine is in such a bad place that I had to leave my job as head of the Reconstruct Ukraine fund. You remember? The position that allowed me to participate last year as part of the Ukrainian delegation. We are now fighting for our survival, and I'm out of the country for security reasons.'

'Where are you now?' he asked, remembering he'd instructed his private office to ignore the emails she'd sent repeatedly over the past months. The voice was impatient and irritated.

'In a small public affairs boutique in Washington DC, which also does a bit of analysis and advocacy.'

'I see,' he quipped with poorly disguised indifference.

The atmosphere between them was strained, imbued with the nasty smell of an old grudge.

Olena glanced at her erstwhile boss. He hadn't changed. Or perhaps he had slightly –more wary, harder. She'd read the news. He didn't have the demeanour of someone who'd handed over the reins. There was little doubt he was still the man in charge. He'd never pass the baton.

'You look on great form, Sir!' she observed, convinced of the enduring power of flattery to provide an instant win. 'This year's annual meeting looks set to be a great one. Every year better than the last, as the saying goes.'

'Certainly.'

The bodyguards were hovering, having understood the moment had come to break up this impromptu "party." They were gently but persistently pushing their principal away from Olena and Olena away from the Don, like sheep dogs herding a recalcitrant flock. It was now or never. She edged a bit closer to her target, fixing him with her emerald gaze. Her voice was calm and polite, and disarmingly firm.

'Sir, can I talk to you privately for two seconds? It's important.'

The Don looked around, hesitant, frowning before grunting a syllable that Olena took to be a 'Yes.' He then added, 'But quickly.'

She leaned inwards, delivering her message to his inclined ear, in a low voice, uninterrupted. It lasted less than 30 seconds but seemed like an eternity to the Don.

They both raised their heads again.

'Fine,' he said. 'Talk to Marissa, my assistant, she'll organise it for you.'

'Thank you, Sir. Much appreciated.'

She turned around and was about to cross the road when the Don suddenly called out, 'What is your plan?'

Olena told him.

*****

That night, Olena headed towards the Fondue House on Talstrasse. It was a special occasion: the yearly private dinner hosted by a famous investor who'd made his money in Russia before fleeing the country in the mid-2000s. He'd since become a prominent human rights' activist, and Putin's *bête noire.* The guest list for his party read like Who's Who because anyone with an interest in Russia wanted to be part of this anti-Putin love-in.

Olena arrived on time, but the restaurant was already packed and the party in full swing. She manoeuvred her way through the crowd towards the bar, greeting everyone she knew, able to put a name to most faces. A few Russian exiles, journalists formerly posted in Moscow, global

CEOs who used to do business there, fund managers who'd made and lost a fortune after Russia's invasion of Ukraine, a sizeable contingent of American and European policymakers, the occasional spook: they were all there.

A voice called out from behind her.

'Olia! What's up?'

It was Sergei, an old acquaintance, a dishevelled economist expelled from MGIMO in Moscow who'd landed a job at the London School of Economics.

'Having fun, gossiping, trading secrets and telling stories! And you, Sergei? What's keeping you out of trouble these days?'

'The same stuff, really: writing reports on the Russian economy for whoever's ready to read them: the EU, NATO, some governments, and you know who...'.

'And? What's the verdict of your carefully researched reports?'

'Russia is f—d. Its economy has been overheating for a while, but the rouble is tanking despite the Kremlin draining more than half of its sovereign wealth fund to prop it up. It's game over. Inflation is up and sky-high borrowing costs mean that Putin can no longer guarantee both guns and butter. Of course, it will be guns, but I only give it three or four years before the economy is doomed. The war economy will have run its course and there'll be nothing left to do, apart from exporting commodities to China. This is Russia's only hope: to become a Chinese satellite. And remember, Olia: there won't be any men left in the country. They'll all be either dead or gone.'

'What makes you so sure, Sergei? Three or four years is a long time. Quite long enough for Putin to create mayhem, to make life impossible for Europe and to reduce my country to rubble. And probably others in the vicinity as well, who knows? I wouldn't feel super comfortable living in the Baltics right now. Would you?'

More guests had arrived, adding to the existent and crescendoing cacophony. The crowd was now so dense that it seemed to move as one, governed by an invisible current.

In a group at the centre of the melee, a good-looking man with a commanding presence was monopolising the conversation, his captive audience hanging on his every word. She recognised Nikolai Brudov, a Swiss American commodity trader of Russian origin who, after having made a fortune in oil and gas, had turned into a "defender of freedom." In her previous life at the Circle and in the investment world, she'd dealt with him on a few occasions. Since then, rumour had it that the nice, principled chap whom she'd known had morphed into an arrogant, controlling and abusive bastard. Olena was close enough to eavesdrop. She noted the condescension in his voice.

'Guys, you just don't get it! Putin is smart. You can put into place all the sanctions you like; he'll always find a way around them.'

One person almost apologetically said, 'But if I may, the EU is doing its best to lean on countries that still allow military goods to reach Russia. These have surely affected the regime, making it more difficult to acquire the critical technologies it needs for sustaining its war.'

Brudov flashed a superior smile, then laughed.

'Yes, that's just it! The EU is doing its best. Fourteen rounds of sanctions. For what? Nothing! Each as ineffective as its predecessor. The EU is a joke. The country that faces the tightest sanction regime in modern history is the one that has just undergone the fastest economic expansion in more than a decade. How do you explain that? Go figure!'

Brudov was in control, shifting his gaze at will, scanning his posse, sure of himself, supremely confident. He spotted Olena and gave her a predatory wink.

'Hi, Olia baby.'

She could take it. Had to take it. She responded with a nod and a tight-lipped smile and moved away.

At the other end of the room, she spotted Phillip Tiddlethwait in an animated conversation with a young woman. Sensing her eyes upon him, he turned towards Olena but then studiously ignored her, almost ostentatiously looking straight through her. She turned away and found herself face to face with her host.

'Hi, Olena, thank you for coming. How are you?'

'Hi, Anthony! Thanks for asking me! I am well and having a great time. I feel lucky to be here.'

'There's a chap I'd like you to meet. I'll introduce you as soon as I see him. He just founded a think-tank in London on Russia's future. It may be worthwhile having a serious conversation with him.'

'Sure, but take your time, Anthony. There is so much noise and so many fabulous guests. I'll wait for dinner before engaging in the heavy-lifting, more serious stuff. The fondue smells as if it's almost ready, no?'

'Yes, it won't be long now. We're just waiting for Sir Reginald to get here. He's going to say a few words of welcome before we sit down to dinner. He should be here very soon. I am surprised he's not here already; it's not like him to be late.'

At that moment Anthony felt his phone vibrate in his pocket. He took it out and glanced rapidly at the new notifications. Despite the ambient temperature in the overcrowded room, he was now ashen, shock draining the colour from his cheeks. With the mechanical gesture of someone not quite aware of what they are doing, he climbed on to a nearby chair.

Sensing the need, the revellers closest to the makeshift podium called for quiet by tapping their glasses. The clear sound successfully cut through the brouhaha and an anticipatory silence descended on the restaurant.

'Thank you, thank you, my friends. As I think most of you knew, we were to have the pleasure of welcoming Reginald Hubert here this evening. It is with shock and profound sadness that I have just learned that earlier this afternoon, Sir Reginald was found dead in his hotel room in Klosters, having apparently suffered a fatal heart attack.'

A wave of myriad emotions swept the room: shock for all, personal grief for some, morbid curiosity and suspicion for many. Someone suddenly shouted, 'And what's with the "apparently?"'

'I don't know,' confessed the host, genuinely surprised by the question. 'That was the wording of the message; I just shared it with you as was. Don't read too much into it.'

Too late. The genie of doubt was out of the bottle and was already doing the rounds. Among Russian specialists, Reginald Hubert wasn't just anyone, but a living legend. In the 1990s, he'd been the British Ambassador to Moscow; in the 2000s, an adviser to some of the largest Western companies doing business in Russia, before embarking around 2010 on a more sensitive path, serving as a grand go-between for anybody seeking a discrete meeting with a member of the Russian elite. Subsequently, he became an éminence grise and broker to anyone in need of hard-to-acquire information on Putin and his acolytes. Sir Reginald was the consummate super-high-end-mister-fixit for anything labelled "Russia."

Dan Scott, a Democratic Senator Olena knew from Washington, emerged from the crowd and joined her where she was standing together with a group of now much less ebullient party-goers.

'Good evening, Miss Kostarenko,' he said loudly, as if wanting to be heard.

'Good evening, Senator.'

'Or may I call you Olena?'

'Please do.'

He looked about 50. A man of sturdy build with a frank gaze and impeccably cut short white hair. He'd become quite a leading political figure and member of the United States Senate Select Committee on Intelligence after a long and prestigious career in the CIA's Directorate of Operations.

'I think it could be,' he said enigmatically.

'Could be what?' she asked with an air of surprise.

'Could be a heart attack… or not. These days, everything is possible with Putin. It's not inconceivable that Hubert might be a sad addition to the "London Fourteen."'

Olena, like everybody else at the Fondue House that night, knew what the "London Fourteen" meant: a group of suspicious deaths fomented by Russian operatives on British soil.

'What do you think?' asked the senator.

'I'm not sure. I don't know what to think. I hope with fervour it's accidental, but how can I tell and what do I know, even if we have had similar cases as the "London Fourteen" in Ukraine?'

'And in many other countries,' added the politician. 'Bloody Russians! Putin keeps testing our "red lines." Reginald Hubert could well be one of them.'

Eavesdropping by design, some interested individuals had congregated around Olena and the senator. Everybody had an opinion about these famous "red lines" meant to define thresholds Russia should never cross without incurring the risk of significant retaliation.

Turning towards Dan Scott, a British journalist asked, 'Is it true that Reginal Hubert was one of those who negotiated red lines with Russia at the highest level?'

'Who talks about negotiations? You define red lines. There is nothing to negotiate. That's the whole point.'

With that, the senator brought the conversation to an end.

The fondue, placed on the tables just before the announcement of Sir Reginald's death, had cooled, spreading a sour, acerbic smell throughout the restaurant. Most guests were deserting the party, their hearts no longer in it. A few were still around, but the conversations at the sparsely populated tables were running out of steam, grounded by the evening's tragic news.

Olena took a seat. At the table next to hers, Phillip was chatting with a journalist from the *Financial Times* who'd known Sir Reginald well.

'He just turned 75,' she said, 'but he was in great shape. Hard to think he could succumb to a heart attack, just like that. Everyone wants to believe in an accidental death, but don't you think those in the know could suspect a more sinister scenario?'

'Maybe, maybe not. Heart attacks do happen, quite a lot.'

'The Russians are good at poisonings that give the appearance of heart attacks. It's one of their *forte*,' observed the journalist. 'Can't we tell if Sir Reginald was poisoned or not?'

'Is this off-the-record?' asked Phillip.

'Of course,' responded the journalist who thought she knew who Phillip really was.

'We can't tell for the moment. I very much doubt the Swiss will perform an autopsy. They have no reason to.'

'So, what's next?' insisted the journalist.

'When Sir Reginald's body is repatriated to the UK, the authorities will conduct an in-depth post-mortem including an autopsy. If he's been poisoned, with a bit of luck something will show up in the toxicology report, but there is no guarantee. We might never know if our old friend died of natural causes or not, and we won't know anything for a few days at least.'

'Before the end of the annual meeting?'

'Let's hope.'

'If the autopsy concludes that Sir Reginald has been poisoned, wouldn't this be a reckless breach of a major red line?'

'Yes, quite an unprecedented escalation. We'd take it as a not-so-hidden declaration of war', said Phillip.

Olena looked away and plunged her fondue fork into the now over-cooked, coagulating yellow magma. The sweet-smelling Alpine delicacy had turned acrid, much like the collective mood. People were on edge. Her Davos was off to a bad start.

2 – Sunday, 19 January 2025

One more day to go, and the 47th US President would take the reins. For good. Unbridled.

Since the November US election, the Davos crowd had been in the paradoxical state of both overdrive and suspended animation, trying frantically to figure out what to do while not having the faintest idea of what was *really* in store. The bridge between the "what could happen" and the "what would happen" seemed impassable. Nobody had a clue, not even the insiders, perhaps not even Donald Trump himself.

To shed some light on Trump 2.0, McPinley, a prestigious if morally dubious global consultancy, and Dolman Group, an exclusive if morally bankrupt public relations firm, had put together a gathering – a private event by invitation only, shrewdly organised the day before the official opening of the Circle's annual meeting. Theirs was an impressive list of speakers: pundits close to the old and new administrations, business leaders, media moguls, plus the occasional think-tanker. CEOs from all over the world had come in their droves together with a spattering of legacy media leaders, all asking the same question: What will Trump *really* do that affects my bottom line? For some, the question could take a more existential turn: Am I on the list, at risk of retribution? If so, what form will it take?

As guests were entering the big white tent erected outside the Congress Centre, high-decibel discussions were well under way. Opinions covered the full spectrum, starting with "this will be an unmitigated disaster," moving through "in the end it might be okay," and ending with "this is America's greatest chance." Near a Nespresso buffet, a disparate group of attendees had clustered around Dan Scott. The outspoken Democrat was engaged in sharing with them exactly what he thought about Trump.

'If you really think America's biggest problem is China – then, you are wrong!' he asserted. 'America's biggest problem is Trump himself. Just wait for it. Just wait for Robert Kennedy Junior, Tulsi Gabbard, Kash Patel, Musk with his Department of Government Efficiency and all the others to enact their policies; even a tiny fraction of what's been announced is enough to spell disaster. Confirmed or not makes no difference. None of this makes any sense. This is not a group of advisers, but a shock troop battalion charged to lay waste to all the officials and institutions that Trump fears or despises. I warn you, mark my words: as of tomorrow, it will be like a return of "The Avengers," but this time in real life, with real consequences.' He paused a few seconds for effect, before adding: 'Then you'll observe what non-linearity looks like. Small causes producing huge impacts. Cascading effects. Catastrophes feeding into each other. Not only at home, but all over the world. Chaos. I predict total chaos.'

Overhearing this, two prominent American fund managers, big Trump donors, sniggered.

'Loser!' said one, pointing at Dan Scott. 'You've got to understand that you, Democrats, didn't lose the election as much as Trump won it. The American people want Trump. It's as simple as that.'

'Pedantic moron!' blasted the other. 'You have no f—ing idea of what you're talking about. Save your breath – shut it!'

A bit farther into the tent, a large group of Asian and European corporate titans had assembled with some of their American peers. Among them, back in 2021, many had publicly condemned President Trump for inciting the mob that had attacked the Capitol on 6 January 2021 and for supporting the violence and undermining the law. They'd changed their tune, now covering their backs. Last November, they'd offered their enthusiastic congratulations on social media and suggested that Trump's election heralded an era of great opportunity for America. As an aside, they'd also expressed their excitement about working with Trump and his administration. Their earlier principled stance had evaporated like snow in the sun. Who could blame them for not standing up for their own ideals and convictions? It was not a question of being spineless, cynical or opportunistic, but rather the necessity to be responsible. Wasn't it? A tech investor got it spot on: 'That's how it is. We have no choice. We are accountable to our clients, employees, local communities and shareholders of course, first and foremost,' he said, adding, 'We can't abandon any of them, and we must play with the cards we've been dealt. It would be irresponsible to do otherwise.'

How very clever! thought some business leaders in the audience: revisiting "stakeholder capitalism" to cover up their volte-face.

Having listened intently, a European CEO interjected with sympathy: 'In any case, who are we to judge? We understand your predicament, even more so because we may soon find ourselves in the same fix.'

At the far end of the tent, Phillip Tiddlethwait, who had been invited to the private event courtesy of a British banker, sat alone, discreet, but in observation mode. After last year's meeting, his cover had been blown at a great personal cost to the Don. An official Circle invitation – the coveted white badge – was therefore out of the question, but he was much too valuable an asset not to be deployed beyond the perimeter of the Congress Centre, the white-badge-only sanctum. Having been the Don's chief of staff, he knew so much about the inner workings of the Circle and the Davos crowd that it would have been a waste not to have him there. A highly confidential department set up for that occasion, placed within the UK National Security Secretariat, had concocted a role for him, and provided a cover. On His Majesty's Secret Service, once again, with only a handful, back in London and Langley, in the know.

For an hour or so, the event went off without a hitch, short both on surprises and insights. Three groups had emerged among the panellists.

The first was composed of enthusiastic Trump supporters, the faithful among the faithful who'd been on board the MAGA (Make America Great Again) train since the beginning, joined during the journey by a bunch of rich tech entrepreneurs and financiers who'd gone full Trump for business reasons. Buying influence to enact their ideas and policies made eminent sense, and the sweet promise of tax cuts provided the cherry on the cake.

The second group, dubbed the "bend-your-knee-CEOs," was the largest, amalgamating the agnostics and the recent "converts" who'd changed their tune after the November election. They'd done their utmost to look sincere, trying so very hard to put forward a rationale in support of their case, and sometimes even going the extra mile by donating company money to Donald Trump's inauguration fund and making the pilgrimage to Mar-a-Lago to pay their respects. Many had already begun to believe in their own lies, announcing that Trump would do much better than the naysayers thought. For those who'd previously gone public stating that Trump was unfit to govern, a narcissist, a despicable, stupid, ill-tempered, erratic, vindictive individual, an autocrat, a fascist, a carnival barking clown, you name it, the conversion would prove an uphill struggle.

One who'd left no holds barred in his criticism of Trump right before the election showed the way by quipping on stage: 'Sure! I had some strong words for President Trump that I now regret. But I count on his magnanimity. And look at JD Vance: he once called our president an "idiot" and privately compared him to Hitler. Did it do him any harm? Not the least. He is now the vice-president of the United States of America! So, "Sir," I'm waiting for the call!'

The room laughed. Some applauded.

And last, the fast-shrinking group: the few remaining die-hard sceptics and opponents who, against all the odds, despised the new president and abhorred his upcoming policies so much that they'd stuck to their guns. But even among them, apart from Senator Scott, the comments were measured, the attitudes guarded.

In truth, among all attendees, circumspection was the rule of thumb. Everyone in the tent was operating with prudence; nobody wanted to put a foot wrong. Fear was contagious. Why take the risk of criticising President Trump when the die was cast? What was the point? They were all in the business of finding solutions, not whining about values.

At the end of a short break, the moderator announced the next session: President Trump and tech: A new beginning. He called his panel. Three speakers sprung energetically on stage, sure of themselves, at ease and in control. They took their seats, with a fourth remaining empty. Its name plate read "Caspar Munchausen." The brilliant scientist in charge of the Generative AI research team at Paladin hadn't shown up yet.

'Let's start. Caspar will join us later,' said the moderator with confidence before turning to the CEO of one of the "Magnificent Seven" tech companies. 'How will it be for you?' he asked. The CEO went on for a few minutes, spouting platitudes and assuring the audience at the end that Trump's victory would usher in a "golden age of American innovation that would bring benefits for everyone."

'That's quite a turnaround!' retorted a journalist, supposedly to himself, but intentionally loud enough to be heard.

Indeed. A quick Google search, the default response of most conference goers, would have revealed the extent to which this particular CEO had publicly, repeatedly and vehemently criticised Trump, from right after the attacks on the Capitol to the last days preceding the election. Now he was on a tortuous, perilous, uncertain path to hypothetical forgiveness. Yes: new beginnings, for sure, but they'd be harder for some than others. Redemption would not come cheap.

The session went on in the same vein, uneventful, with the three speakers proclaiming in unison the advent of a golden age of innovation for Trump's America. By the time the moderator was summing up, Caspar Munchausen still hadn't arrived.

'Weird,' observed the moderator, slightly disdainfully. 'Pity though. He would have added an interesting perspective.'

No one in the tent seemed to care too much, except for the very few who'd come specifically in the hope of gleaning some insider information on how AI research and Big Tech would support national security in the Trump administration. A big issue, to say the least, and one in which several services had a keen interest.

Phillip, who'd been taking notes on his laptop, then looked around the room, taking in his surroundings. The gathering was imbued with a mix of solemnity and self-assurance. They were witnessing history, which merely added to a certain grandiloquence and an assertive sense of their own importance.

In this crowd, Phillip was conspicuous by the lack of attention he was paid, with the exception of a woman coming his way.

'Are you a summary writer?' she asked.

She was glamorous. A cross between a Miss America and a Fox newscaster, wearing a just-flirtatious-enough body-skimming, cleavage-hinting, black dress. The vertiginous heels completed the look. Everything about her seemed designed to attract the attention of the male gaze. Her long blond hair cascaded in glossy waves, framing her heavily made-up smoky eyes and sharply defined red lips. She looked 40-ish.

'Sort of.'

'Hi! I'm Gloria,' she said vivaciously.

He stood up. 'Pleased to meet you. I'm Phillip.'

He was taller than she'd thought. Good-looking, laid back but sophisticated, athletic, muscular, even. For a moment, she let her imagination run away with her. His slightly floppy brown hair, swarthy unshaven chin, and his dark, sharp enigmatic eyes, called to mind the heroes of the Netflix series she enjoyed so much. He was her type.

'What are you doing here?'

'Same as you. Trying to understand what President Trump will bring.'

'Not same as me, then. I know what he'll bring. Nothing but the best. I'm one of his groupies.'

'Good for you! In what capacity?'

'I've been with him for years, helping with tech in the first administration and having done my bit as a fundraiser to ensure there'd be a second one. And here I am!' she said, with a flirtatious shrug of her shoulders which had just the right effect on her dress.

He should have guessed. Her style suggested a political statement, like *I wear clothes that men like me to wear.*

'You haven't told me what you do here,' she repeated.

'I'm a former employee of the Circle. Don't have your white badge. Don't have a badge at all, in fact. I'm helping some CEOs to make the best of their Davos experience. I'm an adviser to CEOs.'

'Lucky them and good for you! I'll see you around.'

She gave him her card before vanishing into the crowd.

Phillip decided the moment was right. The general hubbub and the constant comings and goings rendered him more or less invisible. He reopened his laptop and tapped out a long alphanumeric sequence. It opened an undetectable partitioned hard drive, with the new screen identical to the standard one. He went into the inbox and started typing, acutely aware of his surroundings.

"Caspar Munchausen, Head of Generative AI research at Paladin, was due to participate in a session this morning at the McPinley – Dolman briefing on Trump policies. As you'll recall, Caspar is best known as the originator of Project Aven, the US DoD initiative aimed at using AI to analyse drone footage and machine-learning-assisted targeting. Many believe Project Aven will eventually lead to the militarisation of AI and new applications of generative AI like autonomous weapons. It is also assumed that this initiative will gain new momentum under the Trump administration. Several of its members have a financial interest in making sure this is the case.

Caspar didn't show up. Investigate asap.

Also provide info about Gloria Nobow, Founder of Fast Tech Capital Partners, USA."

He pressed the arrow and locked the laptop. Generative AI had instantly transformed his note into a neat official memo that only three people in London would receive. Soon, he'd be informed about Caspar's fate, and Gloria's details. She intrigued him.

*****

Nikolai Brudov glanced down at his watch. The Patek Philippe Grand Complication indicated 3.00pm sharp. *I've just got time*, he thought, the shadow of a knowing smile crossing his lips as he dialled the number of his assistant. 'The car, now.'

Two minutes later, when he came down, the four-wheel-drive Bentayga was waiting in the courtyard of the Grandhotel Belvédère. He got into the front and barked at his driver. 'Take me to Serneus, quickly, and drop me on Clavanuovweg 1.'

'Yes, Sir.'

The chauffeur entered the address in the GPS but knew his way. He'd been there before, a 20-minute drive to an exclusive area near Klosters that combined discretion with a few over-the-top luxury chalets. The Russians, when they could still come to the Circle, loved it. Many international oligarchs still did.

Brudov made a call, asking his interlocutor pointed questions about the commodity market before passing some buy and sell orders. Then he hung up, took another mobile from the glove compartment and, using speed dial, called another number.

'Niko here. I'm calling you *incognito*.'

'Hi.'

'Has the *Lupus Power* delivered its cargo?'

'No, not as far as I know. Not yet.'

'Why? What the f—k is going on?'

'Problems with the insurer. It might take another two or three days to fix it. Working on it as we speak.'

'Are you kidding me?'

'No. Doing my best.'

'Not good enough. We must find a solution. I have an idea. Can't discuss it now. Be at the Belvédère for 6.00pm. No, wait. I have a meeting in a few minutes which could run over. Make it 6.15pm.'

They'd arrived at their destination.

'Here you are, Sir. Clavanuovweg 1.'

'I know. Come back in two hours. I'll be waiting for you here.'

He let the Bentley disappear before walking a few hundred metres down the street, towards the forest. He stopped in front of a magnificent old chalet, traditionally constructed in larch and stone encircled by an elaborate balcony carved with floral motifs. It was the kind of place that rented for north of a million Swiss francs during the Circle's annual meeting. Some participants had more money than sense, or perhaps not. It was just that for some, money was an irrelevant abstraction.

He rang the bell. Immediately, a distinguished middle-aged lady perched on a pair of black patent Louboutin pumps and dressed in an iconic Chanel tweed jacket trimmed at the collar and cuffs in gold opened the solid wooden door. She could have been a style-conscious senior partner at a top private bank or law firm.

'Welcome back, Mr Brudov. It is always a great pleasure to see you. Please come in.'

The voice had a slight Eastern European accent, composed but deferent.

'Good afternoon. Happy to see you, too. Same as usual.'

'Of course. We have your booking. The changing room is over there, as you know, and your meeting room is just beyond it. Here is the key. And your kit.'

She handed him a zipped Vuitton keep-all bag. Off he went.

Once in the safety of the changing room, he checked the bag's content. Everything he'd ordered was there: the flesh-coloured head-to-toe latex bodysuit, a collection of different sized dildos, several pairs of handcuffs and some ropes. He meticulously, almost reverently, handled each of the "toys," taking his time, savouring the moment. Anticipation was always the best bit.

He took five minutes and then knocked. There she was, girdled in an ultra-tight black leather dress, her face covered by a carnival mask in the shape of a black raven. She sported a pair of black stilettos that made her look even taller than she was.

'Here he is, my naughty Nikolai!'

Taken aback, he halted for a moment, then murmured submissively through the latex mask: 'I had asked for Katia. Who are you? I don't recognise you.'

'Katia will be here soon. In the meantime, she asked me to take extra special care of you. She told me you've been a very, very naughty boy. On you go!' she ordered, gesturing with an outstretched, highly manicured finger towards the beige nubuck-covered pommel horse positioned in the middle of the room.

'Where is my Katia?' he moaned.

The woman calmly took down a whip from the wall and lashed him once, then again.

'Get on it and lie down,' she commanded.

Brudov obeyed, sprawling longways on to the gym horse. Promptly and skilfully, the woman grabbed his dangling arms and handcuffed his wrists to the pre-positioned metal hoops on the floor on either side of the horse's front "hooves" and then roped his ankles to the hind legs. Hoisting up her dress with sinister efficiency, she mounted him and began caressing his backbone one vertebra at a time, progressing slowly but surely towards Brudov's neck.

'You like that, don't you?'

'Where is Katia?' – the moan had become a whimper.

'Maybe Katia's not coming after all. She might have changed her mind.' As she spoke, she violently yanked his head backwards with her left hand while forcing a small plastic ball into his mouth with the other. Having done so, she threw his head back down with a brutal thud.

'You little piece of s—t. You can't have it both ways. You know that, Brudov, don't you?'

Grim reality dawned, but too late. As best as he could, he started to struggle like a disjointed puppet, able neither to speak nor move. Her skilful use of all his kit had left him entirely at her mercy.

'This is from Mother Russia,' said the dominatrix adeptly applying agonising pressure with her thumbs to his upper neck. 'Remember: from Mother Russia.' His vertebrae started cracking. She loosened her grip. 'You son of a b—h!'

She dismounted and walked round to face him, her cruel eyes flashing above the raven's beak. His back was hurting and, compressed by the bodysuit, his heart was pounding against his ribs, but the physical pain was nothing compared to the terror mounting within. He watched as she moved away, towards a chest of drawers where she retrieved a metal box. Impotent, shackled to his pommel horse, he saw her open the box and take out a syringe. She brandished it with a triumphant gesture before coming back close.

'This is for you, Nikolai Brudov. Another present from Mother Russia.'

He knew he was about to die. Incapable of uttering another word, he passed out.

3 – Monday, 20 January 2025

The Annual Meeting certainly got off to a bang, but not quite the bang the Don had planned.

The opening reception serves as the first movement of the Davos symphony, *vivace ma non troppo*. *Vivace* because it's a stylish, fast-paced and exciting affair, aimed at signalling the unrivalled convening power of the Circle and leaving no doubt that there is nothing quite like its annual meeting. *Ma non troppo* provides the necessary counterbalance: this is not just about offering a networking platform. The joy of reconvening, the thrill of togetherness must be tempered by the seriousness of the task at hand. As the Circle's invitation makes it clear, participants gather with the noble intent of improving much of what goes wrong in the world. This is serious stuff.

The celebratory overture for this 2025 edition had turned into a rumour-mill. Apart from the vintage champagne and exquisite canapés, the only other thing on everyone's lips was the "Nikolai Brudov affair." Of course, not everybody knew him. In fact, very few did, but almost everybody had seen the pictures of him posted around lunchtime on X and Telegram. They'd been promptly taken down, but too late. Like all scandalous content, they'd followed the law of the digital jungle and would now travel far and wide across the social media landscape, immovable, leaving an indelible trace. Nothing was ever lost in the ether. Soon, the whole world would know what had kept Nikolai Brudov from his 6.15pm appointment on the evening of 19 January 2025.

The images were shocking by any standards. Taken from different angles, they showed Nikolai Brudov splayed out on a gym horse, clad from head-to-toe in a flesh-coloured latex bodysuit, a dildo up his arse, and a stack of dollars in his mouth. No one could call them commonplace – but that the incident had occurred in the cloistered confines of the Circle's annual meeting only added to their impact on all who saw them, and on Davos participants in particular. What could this all mean? everybody was asking. As soon as the scandal erupted, the Circle's media team had issued a press communiqué in a desperate attempt to distance the organisation and its annual meeting from the whole sordid saga, hoping unrealistically that "the sad and regrettable affair would not distract participants from engaging in constructive conversations to seek solutions to the global challenges that we collectively face." Instead of silencing the story, the press communiqué had had the opposite effect and only served to add fuel to the fire. In response, questions from traditional and social media were coming at them from all directions. Why in Davos? And why at the time of the annual meeting? Was it a coincidence? Why the dollars in the mouth? Was it some kind of coded message addressed to the Circle? And what was a prominent Circle member and high-profile philanthropist doing in such a compromising situation? Didn't the Circle expect better from its members? Was it true that cohorts of escorts descend on Davos to service the annual meeting? Did the Circle have any ideas about who might be responsible? And did the Circle know whether Nikolai Brudov was dead or alive? It was impossible to tell from the photos. At this point in time, only the police knew, but this wouldn't last long. Already, theories of what had happened were plentiful, mixing facts, fiction and approximation. Rumours were rife.

Anything but impervious to all the above but desperate to preserve an air of control and normalcy, the Don was greeting his guests. Standing in line among them, Olena could overhear the editor-in-chief of a London newspaper, happy to share with a few strangers what he thought he knew.

'My local sources think it's an accident, rough sex gone wrong. It happens more than you'd think. What's more, a British conservative MP who is a regular here told me that Davos is like the annual Conservative Party Conference: sex is omnipresent, everyone is at it.'

'Surely not!' exclaimed a guest in the line-up with incongruous naivety.

'Is it your first time in Davos?' retorted the media leader, scoffing slightly.

'It is. Only in a way, it isn't. I've heard so much about it. It's been my ambition to come for years.'

'Obviously you've only heard the official narrative. You need to come more often and go to a few more after-dinner parties! But to respond to your question: yes, I am sure,' exclaimed the journalist. 'There are truckloads of escorts, male and female, sent from Geneva, Zurich and other places for the "big party." Regarding Brudov, we already have the draft of an article ready for tomorrow morning. As far as we know, he was in a chalet near Klosters rented by a woman who runs high-end escort services. We would have loved to interview her, but she's already vacated the place with her staff. The vast chalet is now empty and the lady nowhere to be seen. I don't even know her name. As for the now-infamous trader. I'm told he's alive, digesting the humiliation in a hotel somewhere in Zurich. Can't go home, poor chap. His wife and children are probably not waiting to welcome him with open arms.'

The queue was slowly moving on, the Don greeting guest after guest with a manner akin to an aloof and self-important senior statesman. The body language left no doubt as to who was in charge at the Circle. Solemn, he stood ramrod straight, a defiant look in his eyes, full of an inflated sense of his own importance. He had a polite, albeit innocuous, word for everyone. Cosmetic changes in the organisation notwithstanding, he was still the top dog. Olena's turn came.

'Good evening, Sir. And thank you again for having me as an official participant. I'm most grateful.'

He extended an icy hand, avoiding direct eye contact. Not a word. He hadn't digested their previous encounter.

Unperturbed, Olena joined a group of former colleagues standing nearby, most likely on call if the Don needed them.

'Hi, guys,' said Olena.

'How very nice to see you, Olia. We miss you at the Circle, but great to see you back with a white badge. Clearly, the Don can refuse you nothing these days,' joked one.

'We are gossiping about Brudov,' said another. 'Did you ever meet him when you worked here? As an investor, he must have been in your portfolio.'

'Once or twice at the Circle and we stayed vaguely in touch in the VC world,' responded Olena.

Some in the group knew him and his entourage. In every testimony, Brudov sounded like a character from a Hemingway or Danielle Steel novel, depending on whom you asked. Handsome, mysterious, ruthless in business, blessed with a sharp mind and quick temper. An icon in the financial world. But the bright trader turned investor brimming with confidence and the generous philanthropist also had a darker side. Some colleagues had described him as impulsive, impatient and unforgiving. A bully and a take-no-prisoner kind of guy. In short, Brudov had been a super-talented and super-successful trader, but he was also a ruthless b—rd. The philanthropy, the pretence of defending freedom, they were just a façade.

A young leadership fellow in charge of "Impact Foundations" surprised everybody when she said, 'I know his wife, Ariane, quite well. She's also a philanthropist, in her own right. She should have been here this afternoon, representing her foundation, attending with a white badge, independently from her husband. Obviously, participating is no longer an option.'

The group looked at her in disbelief. One person remarked, 'Really?! Poor her. What it must be like to live with such a s—t, and now to suffer such ignominy because of him.'

She went on: 'Strangely, Ariane was quite open with me. She confided not so long ago that she was still madly in love with Nikolai and always had been, since she was 16. They'd met at school. They have three young children. It could be she had no idea about his salacious sexual proclivities. The thought that you can live with a person, yet not really know the real them, is weird but not infrequent …'.

'Maybe she simply didn't want to know,' suggested another colleague.

None of this was new for Olena. She now felt she knew Brudov probably better than Ariane ever had. Even though she'd only met him on a few professional occasions, his profile completed by some tail details were in the file she'd read and memorised before coming to Davos. She knew her man.

She carried on through the crowd.

Elsewhere in the reception room, a middle-aged American woman with a loud voice was energetically extolling the virtues of President Trump. She seemed to deliver each sentence as if it were a proclamation, with no room for rebuttal.

'Hi, young lady!' she shouted as Olena passed by, extending her hand. 'I'm Gloria. Gloria Nobow. Join us. We are discussing all the good things President Trump is going to deliver in the next four years.'

'I'm Olena Kostarenko, from Ukraine. Forgive me, but I'll reserve my judgement.'

'Don't spoil it. Soon, your country will be at peace. We have a plan!'

'I've got someone waiting for me,' apologized Olena, 'I must go.'

Gloria leaned forward with an overbearing smile and tended a business card, an over-friendly hand on Olena's shoulder. 'Get in touch for a chat. Will you?'

Olena was making her way to the exit when she bumped into a small group of bankers, some of whom she'd met previously at the Circle. They said hello, inviting her to join their conversation. It, too, was all about Brudov. More speculations, more rumours, more nonsense.

A prominent investor from Geneva offered his theory: 'There are three interpretations. One is the S&M scene gone overboard. Another is a very disgruntled, pissed-off colleague or former colleague in the know about his habits who wanted to extract revenge, for whatever reason. I suspect this can happen, but there is more to the story, which brings me to my third interpretation. Brudov somehow reminds me of Edouard Stern. Do you remember?' he asked around.

Some did, some didn't. Another European financier shared his own vague memory: 'The financial wonderkid, no? The son-in-law of Lazard's president?'

'Exactly! Murdered in 2005, shot four times by his mistress during an S&M bondage session. The same circumstances: the latex bodysuit, the dildo, the dollars, everything! As if someone wanted to repeat the scene with a different cast, under similar but also different circumstances.'

'What do you mean?' asked one of the bankers, perplexed.

'For Brudov, like for Stern 20 years ago, I suspect there could be a Russian mafia connection as well.'

'Mafia or Russian state?' the banker enquired.

'They're one and the same,' replied the Geneva investor. 'So much intertwined that you can't tell them apart, Russia is a mafia state. In Stern's case, the law enforcers looked at the Russian connection because he had several investments over there that had gone sour. Apparently, he was seeking some kind of restitution, but there were a few notorious Russian businessmen upset about this. Violence, not affidavits, was their *modus operandi*. That's why for years, everybody thought some oligarchs had commissioned Edouard's death. In the end, though, and to the surprise of the investigators, it emerged that it was after all just a *crime de passion*. The police showed that the leather-clad dominatrix had done it alone. She was his mistress. She loved him but he'd abandoned her. Killing him was her revenge.'

'What's the connection with Nikolai Brudov then?' asked another.

'There is no direct connection but strange similarities that don't stop at the dominatrix. Brudov, like Stern, did a lot of business in Russia. In his case, on the commodity side. Like Stern, he made a fortune there, and then lost some of it, having made lots of enemies on the way. The meaty bit about Brudov is that, despite the sanctions, he seems to have continued doing business in Russia. They're only rumours, but they could be true. Apparently, like many others of his ilk, he intermediates between the Russians and the Indians, helping them buy Russian oil, which they refine before re-exporting it to Europe, where he steps in again, this time between the Indians and the Europeans.'

The Geneva investor looked at everybody in the group, his gaze lingering on Olena. 'Guys, I want to emphasise that I'm just repeating what I heard on the grapevine. It may prove to be unsubstantiated. Please don't take it as gospel.'

'We won't,' said one of his pals, 'but the truth of the matter is that Brudov was in big trouble and that the Russian connection is the most likely explanation.'

'True,' interjected another banker. 'Think about it. We all know that in Geneva today, just like in the good-old-bad-old days, the Russians do hire hitmen and pretty women to settle 21st-century business disputes. This kind of stuff has always happened and will happen again, in Geneva, in Davos, anywhere.'

He turned towards Olena before asking, 'You're from this part of the world, and you know this landscape. What do you think?'

She smiled, enigmatically.

'Remember the one about the ass, u and me? Never assume anything!' was her reply.

*****

Olena reread the mail to double-check the address: "You are invited to a VIP Roundtable hosting a select group of world-class business leaders and practitioners for an off-the-record confidential discussion on Sanctions and the Russian Economy. We would be honoured if you could attend and give us the benefit of your unique perspective. #FHD2025 – Freedom House, The Promenade, Davos."

Three private security guards scanned her belongings before letting her in. Freedom House, a misnomer if ever there was one, was more like a fortified bunker than the pop-up place that private donors had funded to celebrate "freedom and democracy" while in Davos.

She made her way to the meeting room. It was devoid of any decoration. Six tables in the centre formed a rectangle. Twenty grey office chairs stood behind them. Suspended from the ceiling, fluorescent lights cast a clinical glow over it all. Two frosted windows hinted at a world outside but gave no glimpse of it. This meeting room was in stark contrast to all the others she'd seen until now: lavish, welcoming, expensively decorated; money was no object. In this case, the host was clearly on a tight budget.

Olena looked around. At the far end, guests had congregated at a side table with a large tray that smelled of stale coffee. Andrew Reynolds, the official host, had taken his seat in the middle. Unbeknown to its current occupants, he'd rented the room on behalf of the shell company he'd set up shortly before coming to Davos. He'd done a great job of nesting this company within two trusts across different offshore jurisdictions that offered minimal reporting requirements and no public registries. He stood in for the true owner, confident that no possible link to the British government could ever be proven. As for Olena, she stood behind a different but no less invisible façade, protected by a Russian doll of multiple layers.

Also unbeknown to the invitees, Andrew Reynolds had drawn up the guest list and invited them as instructed by the true beneficiary of the shell company. All this was quite new to him. To diffuse the tension rising in his body, he took a moment to consult his notes and do a bit of discreet breath work.

'Thank you all for coming. Please take your seats. There are name plates. I'm Andrew Reynolds, Managing Partner of Fentans & Reynolds LLP, an all-purpose British law firm specialising in shipping finance and trade sanctions. In particular, we work on complex sanctions compliance and maritime trade. Our topic today is a highly sensitive one, so I count on your discretion, a prerequisite for a candid exchange of views that we couldn't have in the Congress Centre.'

There were nods and knowing smiles.

'May I suggest we go quickly around the table?'

Everyone introduced themselves, keeping it short. Olena simply said, 'Senior Associate at Precise Solutions, Washington DC.' There were legal experts, some CEOs, a bunch of legislators and policymakers, including the senator, Dan Scott, law enforcers, shipowners, an oil trader and several experts. Except for one Turkish oil analyst, everyone came from the EU or the US.

'Excellent! Cécile, could I ask you for a brief overview?' prompted Reynolds, turning towards a petite woman in her late 30s with a perfectly coiffed dark brown bob. She was Cécile Dufour, a recently elected French member of the European Parliament, confident and very much on the ball.

'Certainly. Both the European Parliament and the US Congress think it's time to put a stop to the "blind spot of sanctions evasions," as we call them. They are everywhere, but some regions have a special knack for them. Take Central Asia. Between 2021 and 2023, exports from Kazakhstan to Russia increased by 4,900 per cent, from 40 million euros to more than 2 billion, almost all of it in prohibited products like semiconductors, drones, computer hardware, chemicals. The Americans and Europeans who sell these goods to Kazakhstan know what they are doing, but they decide to turn a blind eye. This scandal has to stop, so my question to you all is: What's to be done?'

'Yes… What's to be done?' repeated Reynolds emphatically, warming to his task. 'We'll get back to this but in the meantime let me share a few words on the oil situation, the one I know best. Since the first restrictions on its oil exports were imposed, Russia has succeeded in assembling a fleet of around 400 vessels that shift 4 million barrels of oil a day and generate billions of dollars a year in extra revenues that end up financing its war in Ukraine. How is this possible? Simple! By systematically using offshore corporate structures that make it incredibly difficult to identify who owns the tankers, who bought them and who oversees their operations.'

He looked around the room. Expressions were attentive, notwithstanding the exchange of an occasional furtive glance.

'Do you have any questions? None? Let me then share a precise example to illustrate my point. Between December 2022 and August 2023, Lukoil, Russia's second largest oil producer, used its shipping arm to finance a venal British accountant who bought 25 second-hand tankers for more than 700 million dollars in total. Each tanker was acquired by a different special purpose company incorporated by the accountant in the Marshall Islands, with a Lukoil subsidiary registered in Dubai providing the funds by paying in advance to charter the vessels. At the same time, other front companies owned by shipping magnates in different offshore jurisdictions were appointed to manage the ships. A bit complex, but superbly efficient. Lukoil ended up owning its own fleet of vessels without ever being identified. That is, until now. It goes without saying that this operation could never have taken place without the involvement and co-operation of crooked accountants, crooked lawyers, crooked shipowners and crooked shipbrokers. Mainly, but not exclusively, British.'

As Andrew Reynolds went on for a few more minutes, Olena discreetly surveyed the occupants of the room. *Which one of you is on "team Russia?"* she asked herself. It would be inconceivable that there wasn't one in the room.

Dan Scott jumped in. 'Since the beginning, these 25 ships have transported some 120 million barrels of oil from Russia. If we use a conservative estimate of 60 dollars a barrel, that makes a total of 7.2 billion dollars in exports. Not bad by anybody's standards, with or without sanctions.'

He pushed back his chair and stood up. 'We must raise public awareness about how the Russian oil and gas sector constitutes a vital revenue stream for the Kremlin. In 2023, it contributed more than 30 per cent to the federal budget, of which a third is currently allocated to the military. How can we accept that?'

'Because of our own hypocrisy,' responded Cécile, the European MP. 'And it even goes beyond Lukoil. In the G7, we have neither the guts nor the political will to address the refining loophole. This continues to go unchecked. In fact, we've increased our imports from non-sanctioned countries. We've taken advantage of this situation by switching our supplies from Russia to third-party countries that now operate as Russia's middlemen merchants. And they've discovered in the process that we don't really care about the origin of the crude used to create the products we sell. As a result, they rely increasingly on Russian crude oil, which in turn fills Russian coffers with hard cash, ours.'

'Good point! Would anybody like to jump in?' asked Andrew Reynolds.

'I would,' ventured the oil trader from Turkey, 'to corroborate what Cécile just said. In the first half of last year, my own country went from being the 14th largest importer of Russian crude oil before Russia's invasion of Ukraine to becoming the third largest. Three Turkish refineries used 1.2 billion euros worth of Russian crude to create oil products that they then exported to G7 countries. In my own estimate, these three refineries alone generate about 750 million euros in Russian tax revenues that the Kremlin uses to finance the war. And you have the same story in Azerbaijan. Despite having plenty of oil, it has dramatically increased its own fossil fuel imports from Russia to then increase its exports to Western Europe. I'm almost certain it is relabelling some imported Russian fuel and sending it along to Europe. Could this be done without the full knowledge of Western Europeans? I doubt it. The truth is: everybody is complicit.'

He stopped. A tense, palpable silence followed. For effect, Reynolds gave it a few seconds. 'Back to my earlier question,' he said, 'what's to be done?'

'I have a simple, yet very effective solution,' suggested Dan Scott. 'Let's draw up a list of all the Western lawyers, accountants and others who take part in these shenanigans, and then let's make it public. Name and shame!'

'Good idea, but there'll be some huge legal issues with it,' objected a lawyer. 'I want to remind you that...'

Cécile's sharp voice cut him short. 'One thing at a time. For the moment, let's not get bogged down in legal technicalities. A public list is a good starting point, but it requires a lot of supranational collaboration. And would we have a list that is strong enough to make an impression?'

'Yes, we would,' said Andrew Reynolds unflinching, glancing quickly at the notes, prepared back in London, that he'd been given for just this moment. 'I have lots. Mont-Blanc Shipping, for example, a shipbroker based in Geneva that has provided funds for some of Lukoil's vessels.'

Olena, from her strategically pre-chosen seat, had her eyes fixed on John Clooney, who'd introduced himself earlier as CEO of Azimuth, a London-based shipbroker. He was feigning detachment yet was listening very hard, frequently sneaking nervous glances at his phone.

'But we need a list, not just one name,' said the French legislator.

'Of course. I can add 10 to the list immediately, and more,' continued Andrew Reynolds, looking back at his notes. 'What about Anchor Marine, Blue Wave Partners, Harbour Nexus, to start with? We also have a list of vessels engaged in this nasty business, like the *Lupus Power* and others.'

Olena didn't miss it: at the mention of *Lupus Power*, John Clooney's nervous blink was almost, but not quite, imperceptible. His tightening grip and whitening knuckles on the arms of the chair completed the giveaway. He was bracing himself for something.

Olena didn't move, her eyes remaining fixed on Clooney, her expression, almost nonchalant, revealing nothing, a mask of calm without. Within, she felt a triumphant flurry of adrenalin, certain that the videos from the cameras and the mics the tech-ops had installed everywhere in the room would later confirm her conviction. The new AI emotion software never got it wrong.

John Clooney was one, but who were the others?

4 – Tuesday, 21 January 2025

That morning, the Congress Centre teemed like an anthill, with colonies of white badges busily scurrying in and out. The bait? Plenary sessions studded with big names, always oversubscribed, never the source of any scoops. But who cared! The lure of sharing space with a head of state or a billionaire outweighed everything else. Reasons differed: curiosity or vanity, plus the ever-present possibility of a serendipitous encounter with one of the good and great present in the room.

That was the participants' dilemma: how to decide between their incessant business meetings and the temptation to take part in a "big plenary." This explained the perpetual motion of the white-badged "termites" running to and from the Congress Centre into town, and back. "So many meetings, so little time" was the curse of all Davos participants.

It was 8.30am, and there was a 10-minute queue at security. Well beyond the average tolerance threshold of the very-far-from-average global movers and shakers who found themselves obliged to stand in it.

Olena had just left her backpack at the cloakroom and deposited her belongings in the tray of the X-ray machine.

'This is such a balls-up!' muttered a greying middle-aged man who was standing behind her. 'This year, I'm an industry partner. Just coughed up 300,000 Swissies for the privilege and I'm still queuing here like a moron. I had to cut short my breakfast with an important client, and now I'm going to miss the beginning of President Milei's keynote. The guy's got cojones. He speaks my language, and I want to hear every word he's got to say! Sweetheart, you wouldn't mind if I just slipped passed, would you?'

'I would actually,' said Olena. 'I'm in a hurry, too. We must admire the Circle for promoting democracy within its ranks. Whoever we are, we queue the same.'

'Bul—ks! I know there is a super VIP entrance on the other side of the Congress Centre, for heads of state and other V-VIPs. Price tag: 600,000 to 800,000.'

Having passed security and escaped the din of the queue, Olena rushed to the session on the Global Geopolitical Outlook. By the time she got there, the atmosphere in the room was already charged and the temperature on the rise. A European CEO and an Asian minister were in the middle of a fierce argument.

'Listen,' said the business leader with a patronising tone, 'without a rules-based order, your country will never reach middle-income status. You need open borders and free trade to get rich, which is what the international rules-based order is all about. You understand?'

'With all due respect,' responded the minister, 'my friends and I are building a different future. We've had enough of the global north writing the rules: do not cross our borders; trade on our terms; reduce your carbon emissions; condemn Russia; stop importing its oil. Do this, don't do that, and don't expect any more assistance from us, even when it's more than morally due like for the climate. I could go on and on.'

The CEO stared at him, indignant. 'Are you saying you don't condemn Russia's invasion of Ukraine?'

'I am not,' responded the minister, 'but I can no longer take your lectures about democracy, human rights and international law. Let me ask you: did you support last year's UN resolutions taken against Israel but blocked by the US? And did you support Tsahal's blood-soaked war in Gaza?'

'Well... it's not as simple as that,' mumbled the embarrassed CEO.

'In fact, it is quite simple, my dear friend. For many of us in Asia, for many in Latin America and for almost everybody in the Middle East and Africa, your attitude smells of hypocrisy. It elicits feelings of double standards. If Russia and Israel are the occupiers, why do you shun one and protect the other?'

The CEO stared out at the room, seeking hypothetical support, when the minister delt him the final blow: 'The global balance of power no longer reflects the actual shape of economic and political might. In the next decades, it will shift from you towards us, the South and the East. It's high time you realise that your system of global governance, your "rules-based-order-only-when-it-suits-you" must change. It must change because it's finished. It's gone! You understand?' he quipped.

'How interesting!' exclaimed the moderator before turning towards another panellist, the new foreign minister of an Eastern European country.

'A question for you, Minister Barbil, or may I call you Anton? Do you subscribe to this vision? And some follow-up questions, all in one go: your president has expressed sympathy for Donald Trump. Are you enthusiastic about his election? Where do you stand? Which side do you take?'

'I don't take sides, only that of sovereignty. Each country must follow the path that it judges to be in its best interests, without taking orders from supranational entities or other countries. It's as simple as that.'

'Is this aimed at the EU, Anton?'

'No, it's not, but I hear the undertone of your question, so let me say it as it is and put it bluntly. I think we need to stop demonising President Trump, like we need to stop demonising Russia and her president. These are strong men who love their country; they are patriots! Who can blame them?'

'Could you elaborate?'

'I'll start with President Putin,' he said, nonchalantly tipping back in the armchair and crossing his legs. 'We must recognise that Russia has legitimate security concerns.'

He went on. The argument was well rehearsed. Olena had heard it 1,000 times before. It infuriated her deeply. She didn't let it show.

As the session ended, many participants rushed to the stage, eager to seize the chance of talking to the illustrious panellists. Olena went part of the way with them. He was within earshot.

'Minister!' she shouted. 'May I have a word?'

Anton Barbil looked her way with an indulgent expression. 'Of course you can.'

'Thank you. I'm Olena Kostarenko, a former employee of the Circle. I now work in a public affairs boutique in DC, compiling a detailed research paper for a group of important American companies on the issue of new multilateralism and what it means for them. What you just said is fascinating.'

'Really?'

'Yes. Irrespective of whether you subscribe to it or not, I've never heard the argument made in such a clear and insightful manner. Might you agree to an interview with me before I complete the work?'

'Here in Davos?'

'Yes, why not? I know how busy you are but if you have half an hour to spare, we could meet in your hotel, or anywhere else that suits you.'

'For sure! It's very noisy over here. Let's do this at my hotel. It's rather small but we'll find a place. If not, in my room. It's quite spacious. Only if you don't mind, of course.'

'Not at all. Wonderful and thank you so much. I'll be in touch. I don't have a card with me. Do you have an iPhone?'

'Yes, I do.'

'Can I air-drop you my details and get yours?'

'Of course.' He took his mobile out of his jacket and moved it closer to Olena's. She pressed the appropriate button. 'Now you just need to accept my invitation,' she said with a broad smile.

He did.

*****

Back at the cloakroom, Olena retrieved her backpack and swapped her ballerinas for snow boots before handing them back to the hostess in a small canvas tote bag, her mobile inserted carefully into one of them.

She left the Congress Centre and made her way towards Davos Platz, walking besides the erstwhile traditional shop fronts, now transformed by huge billboards celebrating global brands. She was nervous. The moment of truth had arrived. She was on the verge of entering a world that, until a few short months ago, had been entirely alien to her. She did her best to recall the training she'd received in Virginia, back in September. A month-long crash course to learn as many rudiments of the trade as possible in as little time as possible. Just enough to acquire the basics in surveillance detection and counter-surveillance, agent-running, spatial awareness, firearms, psychology, body language, hand-to-hand combat, dealing with an interrogation... She shivered. God forbid she'd ever need the latter! Surveillance detection and counter-surveillance had been the most challenging, a week during which she'd made one mistake after another. But now, here she was, in the streets of Davos, released into the wildness. No more errors permitted. She box-breathed and felt immediately calmer and collected, savouring the soothing effect of the dry, cold, pure mountain air slowly entering her lungs, mentally thanking the nameless SEAL instructor who'd given the course. *How am I going to do this?* she asked herself, contemplating her next move.

She knew she couldn't cope with a full-blown surveillance operation out in the open but, in the rarefied atmosphere of the security zone, she felt up to it. The barricaded centre of town was her hedge. Planting two tailers in the most closely watched place on earth was just about possible, but organising a hostile foreign op with the half-dozen agents required to tail her was next to impossible, like having almost silent microdrones equipped with high-definition cameras. That's at least what she'd been told, and she chose to believe it. Any big operation would inevitably attract the attention of the police and the Swiss intelligence services. This boosted her confidence. *I'll be okay,* she kept repeating in her head.

The simplest trick first. She stopped in front of a shop with a large window. Thanks to its reflexion, she could watch her own back, her eyes darting up and down the street. Participants were bustling from one meeting to the next, others were huddled in groups on the pavement deep in conversation, all under the polite yet watchful gaze of the cantonal police; chauffeurs were waiting, bored but comfortable at the wheel of their limousines. The street life of Davos was playing out as usual. She glanced at her watch, looking right and left, as if expecting someone. Nothing seemed out of the ordinary. But that's the whole point, she reminded herself, any good tail operation would always seem completely ordinary. Suddenly, she felt confused. Could any of them be a tail? She'd been taught that everyone

– a white badge participant, a blue badge Circle staff member, a policeman, a driver, a private security guard, a shopkeeper, even a chauffeur – was a potential threat. How to avoid paranoia? She kept walking down the Promenade, repeating the same thing a few times before rushing into Schneider's, as if on a whim. She ordered a hot chocolate at the counter, taking a last quick look at the front door and the pavement beyond before going to the ladies' room. Once inside, having made sure she was alone, she took her jacket off and turned it inside out so it went from grass green to navy blue, raised its collar, changed her hat, put on a large pair of glasses, transferred the Glock pistol with its two magazines from the bag to an outer pocket of a sleeveless waistcoat she kept on under her jacket, and opened the door. Schneider's, a traditional Graubünden eatery, was full. She made her way to the exit and left, walking at a brisk pace in the direction of the Morosani hotel. Twice, pretending to make a call on her mobile, she scanned the pavement behind her in the reflection of the screen. Nobody loitering, no precipitous change of direction, just busy business-like people – the norm during the annual meeting. Although somewhat reassured, she couldn't entirely shift the insidious feeling of doubt seeping into her mind. The stakes were high, yet she was a complete debutante in the delicate art of counter-surveillance. Could she *really* tell whether anybody she'd crossed was a threat? She checked over her shoulder one last time, banished any negative thoughts, and turned to the right a few metres away from the Morosani. The path up was narrow. She was leaving the relative comfort of the security zone. She was on her own now.

Crossing Schatzalpstrasse, she entered the woods and began the real climb, comforted by the important test she'd just passed. She was not being followed, there was no tail. Some of the nervous mental tension abated leaving space for recurring snapshots of the past two days. So much had already happened. She knew the detailed backstory on Brudov by heart, but for the rest she knew so little. Reginald Hubert and Caspar Munchausen. What had *really* happened to them? Were the Russians so reckless as to target two precious Western assets in Davos? Quite possibly. She had no doubt about that. And what about Gloria Nobow? Why did she keep turning up, so keen to make contact? Was Gloria up to something that Olena hadn't figured out yet?

She'd walked uphill in the woods for 20 minutes, at a steady, effortless pace. Nature didn't scare her, quite the opposite. Its regenerative power had done the trick. The silence of the mountains was soothing: she felt well, almost enjoying a fleeting sense of serenity. She walked on, conscious only of the rhythmic sound of her own footsteps skimming the frozen ground until, suddenly, she heard something or someone crunching through the snow up the path ahead of her. She slowed down, tightening her grip on the gun in her inside pocket, trying to walk as silently as possible. Then a branch snapped noisily, closer. She froze. Serenity banished, all her senses now on full alert, trying to make sense of the sounds, muffled by the snow; it was difficult to discern the exact direction they were coming from. Despite the cold, she felt a wave of sweat enveloping her body. The saliva rose in her mouth.

She realised how desperately alone and untrained she was, deprived even of the false sense of security of a mobile to call for help. She stood still, seconds feeling like forever. All of a sudden, barely a few metres away, their eyes locked. It was a young deer, even more terrified than she was.

The animal leapt across the path and escaped into the woods. Olena resumed her walk, struggling to get her nerves back under control. She knew she wasn't far. After five minutes, the Garmin the tech team had repurposed for her started to vibrate. She'd reached the GPS coordinates. The hairpin bend overlooking the city was her destination. She box-breathed, and again, and again… slowly regaining her composure. She cross-checked on her wrist: 1710 metres. No possible error. She was seven minutes early. A few metres away, concealed by the trees, she could just make out the sledging run descending from Hotel Schatzalp and, every now and then, she could hear the gentle whoosh of a sledge and the happy voices of its passengers piercing the cold air. Some people in Davos were having fun. *He will most likely arrive from there*, she thought.

Phillip appeared on the dot, emerging from the cover of the trees crossing the run to join her. They hadn't seen each other for 10 days, since their final briefing in a safe house in London.

'Well done – you beat me to it!' he said, kissing her tenderly on the lips, adding: 'You okay?'

'Just about, considering this is my first real mission, but I'm not going to lie to you. It's tough, particularly this last bit.'

'You're doing just great!'

She stared beseechingly at him. 'Phil, do I really need to go through all this for a 10-minute chat and a quick handover?'

'Yes, Olenka. We have no choice. There is very little doubt that you and I are being tailed by the Russians, and probably others. How could it be otherwise? We already had this discussion a few days ago. You know that! Every spook here in Davos knows who we are and is making it their business to know where we are. Plus, too many participants also know us and know about my role last year. Meeting in town would be madness. As much as I'd like it otherwise, we can't run the risk. Believe me.'

'But there are only six of us! With no immunity, no assistance, no lifeline, barely any cover. Alone!'

'Seven. You, me and my five buddies. SAS. All retired but damn good. Try to stop worrying. As for the cover, your white badge is perfectly legitimate. It rings true. My role as an unofficial adviser to some British CEOs as well. There are hundreds of people in Davos without a badge doing the same stuff.'

'If anything happens to one of us, no one will come to our aid,' insisted Olena. 'No one will even acknowledge that we're here. Just meeting you is so complicated, and I feel totally exposed walking around town without my mobile.'

'Olenochka, listen to me', he murmured with all the patience he could muster. 'All your devices have been suitably repurposed to avoid detection, but you can never be sure. When we meet, the rule is: no laptop, no phone, no device of any kind. Only your watch. You never know.

And remember, we are operating at the frontier of legality. Only my government knows about this, without any knowledge of the details. If Trump or Tulsi Gabbard ever learn what we're doing here, we are toast. Ratcliffe, or whoever it is at the head of the CIA, would go mad. It would provoke major commotions throughout the US and the UK. We've got to be hyper-careful.'

He took both her hands in his and held them to his lips. 'No one's moved the goalpost, Olenochka. Nothing has changed from the *modus operandi* we discussed back in London. But, if you are having any doubts, you must tell me. It's not too late to change your mind. Nobody, and certainly not me, is forcing you.'

Her pale face was etched against the shadows. They held each other's gaze, her piercing green eyes now displaying a renewed determination.

She hated herself for wavering. Her moment of weakness had passed.

'I'll be okay.'

'Sure?'

'Sure!'

Darkness was falling and it had started to snow. Down below, the city lights twinkled through the flakes.

He held her tightly in his strong arms for a few fleeting seconds before saying, 'We've only got five minutes left before we must get out of here. Two of my guys are waiting for us just over there,' he added, gesturing towards the edge of the forest on the other side of the sledging run.

'Have you had a chance to plant the device in Barbil's mobile?'

'Yes. It's done.'

'That's great and will make the next step much easier, but I need to tell you something: Caspar Munchausen has been found dead, he fell from his balcony in Klosters. Strangely enough, his body was only discovered last night by a neighbour, buried in the snow. It's not in the public domain yet, but it won't take long. Give it until tomorrow lunchtime.'

'My God....'

'Falling from a balcony will soon become the leading cause of death for those who happen to be in Putin's crosshairs.'

'Are you sure it's not an accident?'

'Almost. I'm awaiting confirmation.'

'It's frightening.'

'Yes, it is. Putin is in for the long haul, and he expects that Trump's presidency will be a gift that keeps on giving. If the Russians are crazy enough to eliminate Munchausen in Davos, it suggests they feel confident enough to try to go for checkmate now. We must wait for the results of Sir Reginald's autopsy. If they come back positive, it means that Russia's hybrid war is moving to the next stage.'

'How does that affect our plan?'

'Nothing changes for the moment. We keep going as before. If you could get John Clooney's details in Davos, his hotel and room number, it would be awesome.'

'I'll do my best.'

'And one last thing. About this Gloria Nobow who keeps bumping into us. We don't have much, so it's better if you ask on your own. From what I gather, she's a super-rich heiress from Texas who's been an arch-Trump supporter from the beginning. Her VC fund seems genuine and to be doing well. There is an aspect worth exploring: she seems to have a few interesting Russian connections, in particular with a Russian entrepreneur and socialite called Ekaterina Brutova, who is big in crypto.'

Olena memorised the name and said, 'I'll send a message to Dan tonight to ask if he can help.'

'And if you come across her again and get a chance, stick this to whatever she's wearing,' he said, handing her a small plastic box.

'How does this work?' she asked.

'It's a minuscule microphone, only 80 microns in diameter. It'll stick anywhere. All you have to do is to get it out of the box with a damp finger and pop it where you want it.'

Phillip checked his watch. 'Time's nearly up. There's lots more to discuss but now we need to get a move on.'

They walked in silence the few metres to the sledging run. Two men, sporting heavy backpacks and pulling four wooden Davos sledges came to meet them.

'We're ready,' said one. 'You follow me,' he told Phillip and Olena. 'Paul will sweep.'

Slotting one foot carefully behind the front curved blades, pushing off with the other and holding tight behind, they set off down the slope. Vintage velocity, nose to tail on their sleek wooden toboggans, the rasp of the metal runners filled the silence.

It was now snowing harder, the run barely visible through the flurries. As they were slowing down to negotiate the first sharp bend, a clump of snow falling from the branches caught Paul's attention. At that exact moment, the staccato of an automatic weapon soared into the night sky.

Paul leapt from his sledge, grabbing the UZI PRO from its holster strapped to his chest. 'Keep going!' he shouted to the other three as he unleashed a salvo in the direction of the fir trees. He plunged into the snow while continuing to fire his UZI from right to left.

'Go! Go! Go!' he yelled back over his shoulder to his three companions.

*****

The car stopped about 100 metres from her apartment, on the corner of Büelweg and Spinnelenweg.

'You've got to go, Olenka. It's going to be okay.'

'It's going to be okay? Ugh – after what just happened, it's a question of definition!'

'Olenka, I wouldn't be being completely straight with you if I said a bit of me hadn't expected this, despite all your efforts. Both you and I know the Russians know we are here. Just bloody bad luck that they tracked us to the sledges. Are you sure you were clean? That nobody followed you?'

'As sure as I could be. What more could I have done?'

'Absolutely nothing. And now we're back in the town, we'll be safe, Olenka. Cohorts of soldiers, policemen and spooks from all sides keeping an eye on each other, keeping an eye on everyone else. And my guys are here to look after you. Go, Olenka, you're doing great and you're going to be fine.'

She grabbed his hand. 'Phillip, you have no idea. I'm so nervous. I can barely control myself.'

'Nothing a good night's sleep won't put right. I'll see you tomorrow, to debrief and to figure out what to do next. I'll ping the location.'

'Stay with me, Phil, please just for tonight.'

'You know I can't. Go, Olenka. Trust me it's all under control now. I'll wait here five minutes, until you are safely in the flat. The surroundings are clear.'

She stepped out of the car and disappeared into the darkness of the street.

Less than two minutes had passed before she rushed back in a state of panic and jumped back into the car.

'Someone's been there!'

'Where? What do you mean?'

'In my flat.'

'Are you certain?'

'Yes. I'd done what I was told, a hair in the doorframe. It's not there now! I'm positive. There was someone in the flat, maybe still is.'

Phillip turned to the driver and the man in the back. 'Guys, we need to take a look. Bring your kit and let's go.'

The men both took a large bag from the boot before following Phillip and Olena to the flat. The building was dark and silent. Thanks to a movement sensor, the light in the stairwell flashed on. They climbed the stairs to the second floor and stopped in front of Olena's door. One of the two men applied a thermal imaging camera to it, while the other opened the door with Olena's key, his unlocked Glock at the ready.

He turned on the light. A sparsely furnished, nondescript studio flat, rented by the shell company Andrew Reynolds had set up.

'Wait outside,' said the man with the gun, while the other inspected the galley kitchen and the bathroom.

'Can you check it out?' asked Phillip.

They extracted from their bags a bunch of radio-frequency detectors to sweep the space for any conceivable bug. There were none.

Phillip turned towards Olena. 'Has anything been touched?'

She entered the studio, checked, went around, looked at every possible detail, including the level of her perfume bottle and of the pot of Bircher muesli in the fridge. She inspected and opened the special safe that the ops team had installed in one of the cupboards. Apart from the Glock and its magazines still in her pocket, everything was in it: the repurposed computer, iPad and several mobiles. 'No, nothing as far as I can tell. Everything seems to be in order.'

'Strange. You're certain about the hair?'

'Yes, positive. Phil, I can't stay here on my own. Don't leave me tonight.'

Turning towards her, he sensed her slender body brittle with fear, saw her beautiful face ravaged by anxiety and succumbed to the pleading in her emerald, green eyes.

'Okay, Olenka. I'll stay,' he whispered, knowing he was breaking every rule in the book. Then turning to the two former operatives: 'Thanks, guys, I'll see you in the morning.'

*****

Olena collapsed on to the opened sofa bed engulfed by a sense of relief and longing. Aroused by both the fear and the forbidden, she needed and wanted him perhaps more than she'd ever done before.

'Phil,' she murmured softly, 'come here.'

He lay down beside her and kissed her parted lips. Gently at first, then more and more passionately. At that moment, no one else existed, no mission mattered more than banishing her fear and her doubts. The flicker of vulnerability made her more desirable than he'd thought possible. She'd already taken off her ruby red cardigan. He carefully unbuttoned her white blouse, revealing perfect bra-less pale breasts. With almost a single gesture, he shed his own black jeans and polo. She lay back on the soft feather pillows, glorious, ready. They gazed at each other's nakedness, sharing a suspended moment, exposed, erotic. She flicked the light off. He pulled the white downy duvet over their now entwined bodies. Arms and legs embracing, they listened to each other's hastening breath.

'Olenochka, darling, what's on your mind?' he whispered in her ear.

'You. Nothing else.'

They kissed, caressing each other, without another word.

Slowly, she came upon him, before pulling him into her.

5 – Wednesday, 22 January 2025

Phillip left in the early hours.

Olena, a cup of coffee in hand, reread the encrypted message she'd just composed for Dan Scott, informing him about the latest developments, asking for details about Gloria Nobow, and requesting an urgent meeting. She added in copy the coded addresses of the Senior Intelligence Officer serving the Deputy Director for Operations and another high-flyer at the Agency whose name she didn't know. All in all, these were the only three people in the US who knew about her identity and unofficial existence.

She sent it, pressed a combination of buttons to ensure the message disappeared from the system, entered another password to return to the normal screen, locked the computer and put it back in the safe. She then gathered her things for the day and left for the Congress Centre.

That morning the customary, already high-octane levels of excitement and energy of the annual meeting's hub had gone up a notch. Rumour had it that the 47th US President would in the end visit Davos on Thursday. This, combined with the recurrent rumours about Brudov who'd apparently committed suicide the night before,

Munchausen and the fate of Reginald Hubert, was giving participants plenty to think and gossip about.

Having an hour to spare before her next task, Olena opened the Circle's app to look at what was on offer. The combination of two programmes – the Circle's official one with its 300 sessions and another licenced to the annual meeting's partners with hundreds more – amounted to a veritable tsunami of content. Just too much of it, an oversupply of sessions covering an over-ambitious array of issues. The Don's latest stroke of genius: selling sessions. For the first time in the Circle's history, partners were offered the opportunity to pay for the chance to bring their own content to Davos. *Hats off. Who else would be capable of inviting you to dinner, asking you to supply the food and pick up the tab?* wondered Olena, marvelling at the Don's ability to feed the cash machine with ever more cash. But by doing so, hadn't he unlocked the door of his magic vault and passed the key to the highest bidders?

She scrolled the programme, scrolled, … and scrolled again. It looked as if an algorithmic kindred spirit had had a major hand in concocting the menu. Words like inclusivity, responsibility and sustainability were everywhere, served up in a variety of guises. AI, for example, had to be inclusive, responsible and sustainable. So too economic growth and public policies. While for ideas, their remit was to be bold, catalytic and imaginative. Business leaders: all the above, and visionary to boot. Bingo – double points for the vision! This over-abundance of buzzwords – "thought-leadership, leverage, synergies, disruptive innovation, low-hanging fruit, thinking out of the box, going beyond the call of duty, ...all well-cooked clichés" – proved that consulting firms were probably in control in the kitchen.

More remarkable were the ingredients left out, the absence of what truly mattered. Like an exploration of the complex trade-offs required to solve the environmental and social crises, or a deep examination of what could make growth more inclusive, or still yet a hard look at the reasons why so little had been achieved in terms of tax harmonisation or the suppression of offshore centres. But today these were off topic, off the menu. Had they ever been on it? Therein lay for some the infuriating hypocrisy of the Circle's Annual Meeting: the discussions paid lip service to all sorts of lofty ideals while shying away from the inconvenient radical means of achieving them. Truth be told, the Don had abandoned some time ago any pretence of improving anything, let alone the state of the world.

In the end, Olena decided that the overabundance of choice made her choice impossible and settled instead for a cappuccino in the foyer. In the queue, two white badges were having an argument about who the world "elites" truly were. Sneaking a glance at their badges, Olena realised that she was standing next to a world-famous private equity guru and an equally famous pro-Trump tech entrepreneur. Such was the magic of Davos: engineered serendipity par excellence.

'I get it,' said the financier. 'The election made it clear. We elites must change our ways. We need to take a long, hard look at ourselves. I'm the first to recognise that I live in a rarified bubble that insulates me from what real life is all about for a great majority of people.'

'Exactly so,' responded the entrepreneur. 'I've been saying that for ages. Hence, my support for Trump. He'll pull the elites and their insufferable arrogance down a peg or two.'

'But aren't you a Davos Man yourself?' asked the financier, not without a little ingenuity, a large smile on his face. 'And being a Davos Man, doesn't that make you a member of the elite? Aren't you the elite bad-mouthing the elite?'

'Interesting question! I see myself as out-Vancing JD Vance. I, too, am from a poor working-class family, but JD Vance went to Yale while I went nowhere. I don't have a degree, which makes me a bit of an outlier here in Davos. Nowadays, it is education that confers your membership to the elite club. Without it, but with my billions, I consider myself as a hybrid-elite. There you are!'

'But your billions entirely compensate for your lack of academic education,' pursued the financier. 'Money endows elitism too, you know.'

'Yes and no. Once you've been through it, as I did, you can't erase poverty. It teaches you many things about life that an academic education never will. You've been to an Ivy League university where you learned a great deal about racial inequality, gender inequality, LGBTQ rights. You understand all of this, but what the curriculum omits, and you don't understand, is class inequality. You just perpetuate it. As for myself, I understand it thanks to my background. You can't because of yours. That's your problem. Your university with a multibillion-dollar endowment heavy on greenwashing and woke commitments can't change that. This is why I voted Trump, and you didn't.'

Coffees in hand, the two overachievers stepped away, continuing their conversation, but now out of Olena's earshot. She stayed at the counter, sipping her cappuccino, continuing her observations of other members of the Davos crowd.

Attendees hurried between meetings and sessions, intense and purposeful, engaged in impromptu but important conversations, punctuated by the occasional pressing phone call in hushed tones. Never long, necessarily brief: time was the scarcest, hence most precious, commodity traded in Davos. Operating within a sort of Darwinian food chain, the Circle's key currency, networking, obeyed one elementary rule: keep it short and efficient. There was no interest in networking with someone regarded as inferior in the Circle's value chain. Time was much too scarce for that. So was curiosity. This meant that any attempt to engage in a conversation fast became transactional, with the highest in the pecking order being the one that brought it to an end. No one wanted to network down. Networking followed only one path, with Circle's participants ready to deploy considerable energy to access the next level: up.

Olena looked at her watch: 11.15am. Time to go. She put her empty coffee cup back on the counter where three participants were excitedly sharing pictures on their phones. Apparently, Anton Barbil, the outspoken, overtly pro-Putin Eastern European foreign minister, had been severely beaten in his hotel room the night before. The photos circulating on social media showed him semi-unconscious, shackled to the radiator with a stack of dollars in his mouth.

'What's going on?' asked one of the three. 'It looks like Brudov all over again.'

*****

Olena left the hubbub behind her and descended three flights of stairs, into the bowels of the Congress Centre. There she knocked on a thick metal door that opened on to the offices of Unisys, the contractor in charge of producing the annual meeting.

Over the previous weekend, she'd reconnected with Arthur, a French executive at Unisys in charge of supervising travel and accommodation, one of the many foot soldiers who produced the Circle's annual event. Producing for real, not juggling with abstract ideas and orchestrating grand ambitions as the Don did, but delivering the nuts and bolts: the chairs and tables where participants would work, the sofas where they'd relax, the coffee corners where they'd network, the hotel rooms where they'd sleep, the cars that would ferry them around, the food they'd eat, the drinks they'd consume. In short: a gigantic undertaking, the essential perfectly orchestrated nitty-gritty that underpinned the smooth functioning of the annual meeting. It was hard work that had nothing to do with the programme and its lofty aspirations but vital nonetheless to deliver a successful event. Only what goes wrong gets remembered. Pleasing 3000 demanding participants was no sinecure.

During her time at the Circle, Olena and Arthur had collaborated on a very few occasions, but just enough for her to notice she'd caught his eye.

'Hi, Arthur. I thought I'd come and say hello. It's great to see you again!'

'Likewise, Olena. You haven't changed! How've you been?'

'Very well indeed. It's my first time in your engine room. Do they ever let you out or do you spend the whole week down here chained to that?' she joked, pointing her finger at his computer.

'I'm afraid so. No time to do anything else. A sleepless week.'

'But you can be very proud of yourself. You're the guy who makes it all happen. You are Davos in fact! The only one in town who knows everything that matters about the annual meeting; who's coming, when and from where, with whom, in which hotel, in which room even. The devil is always in the detail – and you've got the detail. Amazing!'

'Yeah,' he said with a mildly satisfied smile. 'It's a big responsibility, and it's true that I'm the only one to have all this info at my fingertips. It's all safe in here,' he said tapping the cover of his laptop.

'Trump's possible visit must have upped the ante for you?'

'Tell me about it. An absolute nightmare. We still aren't sure he's coming, but I had to find 200 rooms for his advance party and had to rehouse six "minor" heads of state and their suite in boarding houses and two-star hotels. They weren't best pleased. But what can I do? The Circle wants Trump, doesn't it?'

'Sure it does!'

Olena placed her hand on his arm, employing the feline charm of her green gaze. 'You and I should have a drink and catch up when this is all over.' Neither the gesture nor the gaze was wasted on Arthur.

'For sure!'

'Then, let's seize the moment,' she said, while unlocking her mobile. 'Otherwise, we'll never do it.'

'Saturday? A sort of celebration when this is all wrapped up. You'll still be around?'

'Perfect. Saturday it is. Do you have my details?'

'Not anymore, I'm afraid.'

'Let me air-drop them to you. Here you go.'

He tended his phone towards hers with a thumbs up.

'See you then'.

Olena left the basement with a sense of satisfaction – duty fulfilled. Back in Langley, the techies would crack this in just a few hours. Before tonight's meeting, the whole alphabetical, internal participants' list would be theirs. It would just be a case of checking the 'Cs.'

*****

Olena left her flat in the direction of the Congress Centre, taking the footpath at the bottom of the building to avoid a possible car tailing. By the time she'd reached Bündastrasse, she was moving with a careful rhythm, adjusting her pace, alternating between brisk strides and a casual amble. On two occasions, she turned into a side street, using the "reflection-in the-window" trick to check for signs of a tail. There seemed to be none, except for the man who, at every corner, was coming a little closer. After crossing Dischmastrasse, she turned left, the third side of a triangle, heading away from the town centre, backtracking on her original direction. At that time of night, the road was deserted. She resisted the urge to glance back, moving fluidly, like a shadow, until Mattastrasse was in sight. She started to walk faster, leaving the town behind her. It took her just a few minutes to reach the muleteers' trail that leads to the Dischmatal valley. She'd barely set off down the path when she turned around and saw him, striding towards her, casting an elongated silhouette against the wall of a barn in the wavering light of a lantern hanging from the beam.

'Hi, Paul.'

'Hello, Miss. I think you've come alone. Hard to be 100 per cent sure, but I feel good about it this time.'

For a moment she took in his appearance and was reassured. A man of about 40, neither tall nor short, stocky, with a benevolent but resolute face, and a quiet intensity in his eyes. Like the day before, he was carrying a large rucksack over a down jacket bulging with the weapons it concealed.

'Thank you, Paul, for yesterday. You saved our lives.' The words, sincere, sounded false. She felt awkward.

'It's okay, Miss. Just did my job. We've got two kilometres to walk and less than 30 minutes. Just follow me, leaving about five metres between us. Something bothers you, you shout.'

Paul, a man of few words, was moving through the night in hushed silence, with the grace and calm of a predator. He projected the impression of someone at ease wherever he might find himself – a bustling city, a desert, the jungle, a mountain. Olena, glad not be alone, trusted him. His calm sense of control was contagious.

The night was clear, lit by a waning crescent moon still casting enough light to conjure silvery shadows that outlined the surrounding peaks. The crisp air accentuated the spectral brilliance of the snow. Here and there, old barns emerged from the trees. In the distance, well above the muleteers' trail, a faint light twinkled through a small window.

Paul left the path and turned right, going straight into the mountain, his feet sinking into deep snow. They were heading towards that light. After a few minutes, they reached a clearing in the forest, with an old barn at the far end. Theirs were the only tracks. As they came closer, a man equipped with night vision goggles appeared out of nowhere and led them to the barn. Two men guarded its entrance and a third stood on a rock above it, a submachine gun on his lap. Paul opened the door and simply said, 'They are upstairs, waiting for you.'

Olena climbed the miller's ladder into a large, dimly lit room that took up the entire surface of the building. In a corner, an old stove was burning. Next to it, the two men were seated at a large table.

Dan Scott stood up.

'Welcome to our Davos safe house. Not so easy to get to, but picturesque – and safe.'

'Hi', said Olena, taking off her jacket.

'Take a seat,' said the senator, immediately getting down to business. 'Without the shadow of a doubt, I can assert two things. First, the Russians are using the Circle's gathering to move to the next stage of their hybrid warfare. One step up. Second, they are after you guys. Let's begin with the latter. What's your reading of yesterday's attempt on your life?'

Phillip glanced at Olena for a few seconds and said, 'Your two points are intertwined, Dan. The Russians tried to eliminate us precisely because they've moved to the next stage of their hybrid warfare. One determines the other. It means that from now on, gloves are off, and everything is permissible from their perspective. No more limits as proven by the fact that even an official British operative like me is now fair game for them. It's a huge step. Makes me think that last year was just a rehearsal for Putin. Very concerning.'

'I agree. They are escalating,' Dan pointed out. 'Dangerously. You agree, too, Olena?'

She nodded.

Phillip went on. 'Regarding their failed operation of yesterday and trying to understand it, we can only work with what we've got. For an op like ours, of this scale, there should be several dozen of us in Davos, plus all the tech and operational support we need. But I understand our constraints and the fact we must operate on a shoestring. Obviously, one of us made a mistake, otherwise they wouldn't have been able to track us up the mountain. I reached our meeting place with two of my guys. They are among the best and I think we came clean. For you, Olena, it's different,' he said observing her eyes. 'Operating with so little support constitutes a huge disadvantage and is mentally draining.'

The young Ukrainian straightened on her stool, her hands clasped on the table, her head held high. Even in these moments, she managed to be elegant and composed.

'Yes, it could be me. I'm the novice here and I could have made a mistake, but I thought we'd all agreed that an effective hostile tail in the security zone was highly unlikely.'

'Yes, highly unlikely but not impossible,' corrected Phillip, before adding, 'The long and the short of it is we were very lucky with the weather. By the time we were sledging down, it was hard to see anything with precision. Luckily for us, the shooter couldn't see much at all. Also, the way the ambush was carried out shows that it was organised on the go, without any preparation, which is kind of a relief in terms of the next few days. It could have been just one person. That's what Paul thinks, anyway. After the shots were exchanged, he went further into the woods and couldn't see more than a single track in the snow.'

'From your perspective, what's next?' asked Dan.

Phillip looked at Olena. Her composure holding, her mask in place, the look that came back at the two men was glacial. Still f—ing terrified – yes. Was she going to show it? Absolutely not.

'I'm speaking for the two of us,' he said, casting an uncertain glance at his companion. 'We have zero chance of finding out any details about this hostile op. We only know that they know about us, but how much? Do they know about our black op? Have they figured out something? If so, how many people do they have? And what sort of means can they mobilise? Is it SVR or GRU? Remember that we are playing defence here. My take is that they can't do much in Davos itself. Risks for us are limited there, even if I can't figure out why they visited Olena's flat. My hunch is that we stick to the original plan. We are doing okay so far. No reason to change tack.'

Dan inhaled deeply, tipped backwards on his chair, hands crossed behind his head, staring at the ceiling and then at the flickering flame in the stove.

'Running such a black operation, blacker than black, means that we are obliged to move forward with our hands tied. After what happened yesterday, we should request massive support, but we can't. Asking for anything would immediately arouse suspicion. If I were to turn to our two guardian angels in Langley, they'd tell me to f—k off and would then immediately suspend the operation. It's a non-starter.'

'But we'll never manage with only my guys,' observed Phillip. There are only seven of us, Olena included. It's not enough.'

'Plus me,' Dan pointed out.

'Yes, plus you. But running the op is not the same as being operational.'

'Quite right. This is why I made the decision last night to bring in my own team of retirees. Same kind as yours, Phillip. All former Ground Branch high-end special operatives involved in our nastiest black ops who now work as private contractors. You saw three tonight; there'll be three more tomorrow, flying in from the Middle East and Eastern Europe. Six in total. I know them all from my time in Europe and Russia. Entirely reliable and entirely deniable if something goes wrong. That makes more than 10 on the ground. It goes without saying that none of our ex-CIA and MI6 colleagues present in Davos for official business can be any help. None knows we even exist. I'll keep coordinating here and will liaise with our two bosses in Langley. By the way,' he added for the benefit of Olena, 'interesting stuff about Gloria Nobow. More on that later. Let's now turn to —'

One of the guards rushed into the room without knocking before he could finish his sentence. They immediately knew something was wrong.

'There is an intruder, or several, on the property. We have sensors all around. One just blipped.'

'Could it be an animal?' asked Dan.

'Could be, but you'd better go downstairs to the backroom until we can OK the situation.' He turned the light off and disappeared.

They'd just had time to feel their way down the ladder in the dark and take refuge in a small annex-like room at the back of the barn before the noise of gunfire erupted. From inside, behind a gnarled wooden door, they could discern the rapid exchange of automatic weapons fire muffled by silencers, sometimes punctuated by the crack of handguns and the odd bullet impacting the barn's ancient planking with a splintering thud. It all lasted less than 30 seconds, during which the three of them remained crouched without a word, their Glock 17s in hand, all senses on high alert. Then nothing. Occasionally, they could hear the murmur of their colleagues talking to each other on a two-way communication system. After 10 long minutes spent in a sticky silence, Paul came in.

'It's all clear. There were three of them. We wounded two, maybe killed one of the two. They escaped on a skidoo equipped with a trailer positioned on a mountain path a few hundred metres behind the barn. I think our numbers caught them by surprise. We didn't chase them, not knowing how many more might be out there.'

Dan stared at Phillip and Olena, a long, appraising stare. 'One of you must be bugged. It's impossible otherwise. We ran a check on the barn before you arrived. It was clean. Sabina!' he called out, 'bring the equipment.'

Immediately, a 30-something, slightly dishevelled operative stuck her head through the doorway. She came close and extracted a small radio-frequency detector from her bag, directing the micro-pointer antenna towards Phillip and Olena. After just a few seconds, she pointed to Olena's sleeveless Patagonia waistcoat.

'It's in here,' she said. With adept fingers, she retrieved a miniscule piece of metal the size of a large pinhead from one of the plume-filled panels at shoulder level of the offending garment. She examined it.

'A GPS tracker, most likely powered by a strontium battery. Good enough to send a more or less reliable signal in and around Davos for a few days.'

'My God!' exclaimed Olena, clasping her hands to her mouth with a gasp of horrified disbelief.

'A month's training is never enough,' said Dan, before asking, 'Where do you think you picked this up?'

Olena pondered for a few seconds, remembering with a shudder that despite the collective body heat at Monday night's reception, chilled by the stress of it all, she'd kept her waistcoat on.

'Gloria – she beat to me to it! It can only be Gloria Nobow.'

6 – Thursday, 23 January 2025

At half past midnight, Dan Scott came back to his hotel to find a voice message on the mobile he'd left in the safe. A call from the Don himself, inviting him to participate in a confidential meeting at 8.00am that morning aimed at shedding new light on the accidents that had taken place during the annual meeting. If he had any question, the Don was suggesting Dan call him back directly on his personal mobile, any time before 1.00am.

Dan composed the number, and the Don responded immediately.

'Caius Schwenk, here.'

'Good evening. This is Dan Scott. Sorry for calling so late, but I just found your voicemail. I'm intrigued. In principle, I'd be happy to participate, but it depends on who else will be there. That said, I'm not sure I can bring much to the conversation. Please tell me a bit more about what you have in mind.'

'Senator, I have no doubt you must be present. Don't be too modest. With your background and current responsibilities on the US Senate Intelligence Committee, you'll have much to contribute.'

The voice was confident and purposeful, with a strong, guttural accent.

'I must tell you,' pursued the Don, 'that I am very concerned by the inexplicable accidents that have happened over the past days and by the distasteful photos that seem to relate to them. All this tarnishes our reputation. Before President Trump arrives in Davos later today, I would like to hear from some of our most valued guests what they think is going on.'

'Who'll be there?' asked Dan.

'Only exceptional and trustworthy people like yourself. All very senior white badges from NATO countries, plus the head of the Swiss Federal Intelligence Service and the commander of the Graubünden cantonal police, which is, as you know, in charge of our participants' security here in Davos and of the ongoing investigations. My assistant will send you the finalised list of participants tomorrow morning at 7.00am. I hope to see you at 8.00am in my office in the Congress Centre. The meeting will remain confidential of course.'

'I'll confirm once I've seen the list. Thank you, Caius.'

'Thank you, Dan, and good night.'

*****

If the meeting was supposed to take place below the radar, it didn't. The Don couldn't help wrapping most of what he did in a certain pomposity. A posse of private security guards and Circle employees hovered around the suite of rooms that made up his private office, ushering participants one by one into the elegant meeting place. At its entrance, the Don, flanked by his compliant and long-suffering number two, ceremoniously welcomed them as if they were attending a meeting of the UN Security Council or the G20. It was all a bit too much, but it pandered to his self-importance and made him feel good.

Inside, everything had been meticulously prepared. Thermos flasks of coffee and tea as well as pastries and fruit baskets graced the oblong table. Name plates had been pre-positioned at each chair. The Don took his seat at the head of the table and invited his 12 guests to do the same.

'Good morning, dear friends and participants, and a very warm welcome to you all. Thank you for finding the time in your already overburdened schedules to join me this morning for what I consider to be a vitally important meeting. As I am sure you are all aware, a series of unfortunate accidents and disgraceful postings on social media have recently taken place. They have nothing to do with our annual meeting, but most journalists don't see it that way, and many of our guests are asking questions. Therefore, before I have the privilege of welcoming President Trump later today, I would like to pick your brains on how you see things. I want to better understand what's going on and benefit from your perspective.'

He cast a quick glance around the table and got an immediate sense of the unease permeating the group. This was an unorthodox situation. These were all senior decision-makers from the world of defence, diplomacy and intelligence, not in the habit of sharing insights or secrets with anyone and especially not on command. Why would they give anything away to the Circle? It didn't make sense, but they were all there, such was the talent of the Don: an aptitude for personally convening individuals a notch or two above his rank. The art of networking "up" for which the Circle was renowned came from the top. Even so, this was going to be a challenge.

'Could you be more specific?' asked a senior NATO official. 'What's troubling you and what has all this got to do with Trump? What precisely do you need from us? What's the point of this meeting?'

'Of course. Let me run through the details,' reacted the Don, suppressing with difficulty a toxic mix of anger and humiliation welling up. He'd built his career by unflinchingly showing deference to his guests, never upsetting any one of them, but he was not used to having his authority questioned with such bluntness and, what's more, in full view. He took the blow, looking at his notes.

'I think there is a pattern here. All these events appear to be related, but I must emphasise once again that none of them took place during the official annual meeting. It all begins on Saturday, 18 January, two days before the opening, with the heart attack of Reginald Hubert. Some parts of the media are peddling the notion that it was a cardiac arrest made in Russia. We don't know and hope this is not the case.'

Dan Scott, imperturbable, surveyed the room. At this moment, he alone, he thought, knew that Sir Reginald Hubert had indeed been poisoned. Earlier that morning, Phillip Tiddlethwait had sent an encrypted message to inform him that initial toxicology tests on Sir Reginald's body had found nothing suspicious, but that a further test performed by an expert botanist had shown in his stomach traces of Gelsemium, a rare and deadly plant toxin known as "heartbreak grass," because its leaves, if swallowed, cause cardiac arrest. Not that he needed a reminder, but in his message, Phillip also mentioned that one of the "London Fourteen" – Alexander Perepilichnyy, an exiled Russian banker – had been murdered with Gelsemium back in 2012. Phillip concluded by explaining why the UK government wanted all this to remain confidential for a few more days. Further tests would be performed to confirm the Gelsemium hypothesis and the British Prime Minister needed a bit of time to reflect and decide how best to respond to such a dramatic escalation of Russia's offensive.

'Then,' pursued the Don, 'we have the unfortunate accident or defenestration of Caspar Munchausen, followed by the despicable pictures of Nikolai Brudov and his subsequent suicide in Zurich, the vile attack on Minister Barbil and, late last night, an assault on one of our participants, John Clooney, in his hotel. Perhaps details of this latest atrocity haven't reached you yet, but the commander of the Graubünden cantonal police, who is here with us,' said the Don gesturing to a man in uniform seated across from him at the table, 'informed me late last night. Someone threw concentrated hydrochloric acid at Mr Clooney as he was entering his room. He was lucky it missed his face, but it did severely burn his chest. He seems to be in a state of complete shock. In his statement to the police, he says he can't think of anything justifying such an attack. He suggested that it might have been a case of mistaken identity.'

'Didn't he scream? Did nobody in the hotel hear anything? How can that be? In Davos with such security?' asked a participant.

'There are aspects of the incident that we also find strange,' intervened the police commander in a heavily accentuated German accent. 'Much suggests that this could only be the work of professionals. There was no fight. Someone might have constrained Mr Clooney to prevent him crying out as another person was throwing the acid at him. But then, why miss the face? Something doesn't add up in this scenario. He was staying in a guesthouse outside of the security zone with no surveillance cameras within the building, and Mr Clooney is so shocked that he seems incapable of remembering anything. The investigation will be difficult.'

'Are we certain of foul play in the case of Munchausen? It's not an accident?' asked a European minister of defence.

'No, it's not. We haven't gone public yet, but we will soon open an investigation for murder. The autopsy reveals signs of a ligature on his neck that could suggest strangling. He also had a cut to the back of his head. All this before falling.'

None of those seated around the table showed the slightest sign of surprise. To all of them, it seemed so obvious.

The Don spoke up again. 'I want to share this with you. Following consultations with my colleagues, I see a maritime and sanction thread in all this. Mr Clooney is a shipbroker. Mr Brudov was an oil trader and, before becoming foreign minister, Anton Barbil was, and may still be, the owner of a fleet of tankers in the Black Sea.'

'And what about Munchausen?' asked another participant with thinly veiled sarcasm, 'Is he in the oil business as well?'

'Of course not,' responded the Don, turning in vain towards the head of the Swiss Intelligence Service, whose gaze was fixed on the wall beyond. 'I'm just offering a conjecture, and observing that in all four cases, I'm leaving Sir Reginald Hubert aside, Munchausen, Barbil, Clooney and Brudov, it's tempting to see Moscow's hand. You are all Russian experts of a kind,' he added with an almost conspiratorial glance at his guests, before asking with theatrical gravity: 'Do you think the Russians are after us here in Davos?' Then, pausing a second: 'Maybe even after me because of what I represent and because of my decision to break my relationship with Vladimir Putin after his invasion of Ukraine?'

A Davos regular, a foreign minister from a Baltic republic, smiled at this delusional remark. *Typical Caius. An inflated ego – always more interested by what he perceives as his role in events than by the search of the truth*, he told himself, looking around the room. Most faces were feigning neutrality. He decided to go first.

'What do you think is happening, dear friends? I'm part of the chorus of Cassandras who've been sounding the alarm for years. If you don't share a border with Russia, what I'm going to tell you is difficult to acknowledge, politically inconvenient to admit and economically costly to accept. It is, however, the duty of any politician who cares about Europe to recognise this grim reality: we are at war with Russia. You can call it hybrid, shadow, undeclared, grey, whatever, but everything points to war in all but name. Your reluctance to call it as it is,' he added, turning pointedly to one of his German colleagues, 'comes from years of complacency on security in favour of energy deals and trade.'

'But if I may,' interjected the Don's number two, 'does that necessarily make Russia the perpetrator of the five accidents listed by Professor Schwenk?'

'Not necessarily, but highly likely,' pointed out the senior NATO representative. 'The Russians are taking advantage of the convening power of the Circle and the high visibility of its annual meeting to escalate. Putin is cornered and has no choice. A BBC journalist once described him as "a car with no reverse gear and no brakes, careering down the highway, accelerator pedal stuck to the floor." That's exactly what's happening here in Davos, and I can't think of a better description to helps us grasp what lies ahead.'

A Western European senior intelligence official, looking pointedly at the Don, went further: 'In my 40 years in the intelligence profession, I've never seen the world in a more dangerous state. Putin is unhinged, emboldened. Just consider what he's doing here at your annual meeting. Blatantly crossing so many red lines – not so long ago, this would have been inconceivable. Not anymore. When you have Trump on stage this afternoon, you must give us a chance to publicly tell him that if he allows Putin to succeed in reducing Ukraine to a vassal state, Putin will not stop there, and our European and transatlantic security will be gravely jeopardised. I concur with our colleague from the Baltics: the cost of supporting Ukraine is high, but the cost of not doing so would be infinitely higher. If you give us a chance during his speech, one of us will seize the opportunity to tell President Trump as much.'

Dan Scott stood up, a habit of his when conveying an important message. He, too, looked at the Don sternly. 'If the topic comes up in the conversation between you and Trump, tell him that what's happening in Davos has a name: "Death by a thousand cuts." It works by exploiting the large spectrum in between war and peace. We are no longer at peace, but it's not quite out-and-out war yet. Well, war in the traditional sense. A very grey zone. The Russians are damn good at it.'

The Don arched his eyebrows, quizzical, as if he didn't understand what the senator was getting at.

'You mean: the five accidents here in Davos are an example of your "Death by a thousand cuts" theory?'

'Precisely. When taken independently, they don't mean much, because they only make sense when you realise that tiny, isolated incidents to which you do or don't pay much attention are part of a well-orchestrated campaign.'

'Perhaps some precise examples would help us to understand. Might that be possible?' asked the Don's number two.

'Of course. I'll start with the most notable ones: the sabotage of two undersea communication cables in the

Baltic Sea back in November. A Chinese ship with a Russian captain at the helm passed over two cables on two consecutive days at the very moment they were severed. Coincidence? No, because it happened again at the end of last year when a Russian oil tanker, part of the Kremlin shadow fleet, damaged five cables with its anchor in the Gulf of Finland.'

'Never a coincidence,' opined the NATO senior official.

'This is what "Death by a thousand cuts" means,' continued the senator. 'Hundreds of tiny and not so tiny incidents weaponizing civilian assets, targeting our critical infrastructure, provoking multiple system failures. Each quite simple in terms of execution but sophisticated in terms of impact. Think of the underwater cables. You use a merchant ship, you find a reason to drag an anchor, bad weather will do, and the job is done. Low cost, low tech, highly effective and easily deniable.'

Dan sat down and the Western European senior intelligence official spoke up again.

'All European military and intelligence agencies now see an escalating Kremlin campaign of attacks aimed at destabilising us. Russian intelligence services have gone a bit feral, frankly. Throughout the continent, we are now seeing acts of sabotage of aircraft and critical infrastructure, plans to assassinate nationals like the boss of Rheinmetall, the German defence company, covert election interference in Romania and Moldova, and an endless series of assassinations of all those who happen to be in the Kremlin's way, or inconvenient loudmouths no longer useful to the authorities. I think this fits with what you called earlier a "pattern of accidents" in Davos,' he said, looking at the Don. 'There is no longer one front line. They are multiple, all over the place, and Davos is one of them. The complex web of systems that underpin our modern societies is up for Russia's grabs. Welcome to hybrid warfare. Welcome to Davos 2025. Wake up, Mr Schwenk!'

'Um,' said the Don, pinching his lip, overwhelmed by what he'd just heard. Sitting on the fence was becoming harder, and more and more uncomfortable. Deep down inside, he had a strange feeling – a bizarre mix of power and meaninglessness.

A former director of the MI5, who happened to be sitting next to Dan Scott, leaned towards him and whispered: 'There is something not quite right in all this…'.

'What do you mean?' asked Dan, with a look of surprise.

'Admittedly, the GRU can be quite clumsy sometimes, but I can't understand why they killed Munchausen but not Brudov, Barbil and Clooney. Three misses… probably too many to be explained away by incompetence, no?'

The senator gave her a quizzical look.

*****

As the Don returned to his office accompanied by his number two, he found Marissa, his assistant, uncharacteristically agitated.

'So sorry to disturb you, Sir, but Olena Kostarenko is outside at the door. She wants to talk to you urgently and she says she won't leave until she's done so.'

'Shall I talk to her?' offered the number two.

'No, better if I do,' said the Don. 'It won't take long.'

He sat down at his desk behind the glass partition. Marissa showed Olena in, then closed the door.

Sitting at her desk, she couldn't hear the conversation but could catch glimpses of her boss, unspeaking, his facial expression moving from mild irritation, through to superciliousness, to resignation. Olena, by contrast, seen from the back, sat bolt upright, poised, and doing all the talking.

After barely two minutes, the Don called his assistant in. 'Please inform Trump's party that Miss Kostarenko will be at the V-VIP door with me and the other members of the Circle's delegation when President Trump arrives at the Congress Centre.'

'Thank you so much, Sir. This means a lot to me,' said Olena before leaving.

*****

A seemingly never-ending motorcade of vast SUVs preceding darkened limousines followed by vehicles bristling with aerials, and another round of SUVs plus a few heavily armoured cars in their tail, filed past the V-VIP entrance to the Congress Centre in the heart of Davos. Finally, a black vehicle that looked like a fortress on wheels stopped in front of the Don.

President Donald Trump emerged from it, distinguishable at a distance by his trademark red tie and golden hair. He paused briefly at the door's threshold, surveying the Circle's welcoming line-up with a measured squint. Flanked by an army of advisers and security, his gait was determined and cocksure. It all felt less like an arrival and more like an incursion to be followed by a victory. *Veni, vidi, vici.* The 47th President of the United States of America appeared ebullient, and triumphant, more hyperbolic than ever. He had every reason to be. The majority of the Davos crowd now adored him. Those who didn't had nonetheless hedged their bets and paid their respect, in one form or another. What was there not to like for the US President?

The Don took a few steps closer, his hand outstretched.

'Welcome back to Davos, Mr President. We are very proud to have you with us again.'

'Happy to be here, Mr Schwenk. The Circle is one of my favourite events. Some of my people, like Vivek, don't like it at all, and Elon never, ever came, but I think you do great. Elon? Where are you?' he asked to no one in particular. 'Ah Elon, come near. I was just telling Mr Schwenk that we are going to make his annual meeting great again, even greater than it is! Let's do the next ones in Mar-a-Lago or one of our beautiful resorts.'

The president laid a paternal hand on the Don's shoulder, and added, 'Mr Schwenk, you'll be amazed by Mar-a-Lago. The very best resort in the world. Truly amazing. You'll love it there. Much better than Davos. Everybody wants to come to see me there. A real power centre. The centre of the universe. Not doing Davos in Mar-a-Lago would be a mistake, a very big mistake, Mr Schwenk.'

The Don smiled sheepishly, lost for a response. The best he could manage was a sycophantic, 'Thank you, Mr

President,' followed by, 'May I introduce my wife, Birgitta, my CEO, Mr Berden, our representative in the US, Mr Cox, the Mayor of Davos, Mr Werner, a former colleague, Mrs Kostarenko.'

'What you do is amazing,' said the president, shaking hands mechanically while looking at the Don. He had a quick appreciative look for Olena and went on. 'So many different people, you have. You're sort of amazing. I have a very special sense for amazing people.'

'Thank you, Mr President. Very kind of you.'

Looking back at Olena, the president told the Don: 'You seem to employ terrific people, top people, the very best,' then in a low voice, pointing his finger towards the young Ukrainian: 'Are all Circle employees as attractive as your assistant? Great girl. She seems gifted. I have a special sense for gifted people. I've seen her eyes. Great eyes. Great green eyes.'

'We do have the best talent at the Circle, Mr President. Now, if you'll allow me, may I take you to the speakers' lounge in the plenary hall?'

Following in the Don's footsteps, the US President said, 'I want to say hello to Milei. I hear he's here as well. Great guy. Very impressive. An amazing patriot. A courageous man, very committed. He's going to make Argentina great again.' Turning around, wagging his finger in their direction, he said to his unquestioning entourage, 'Do you know that Argentina was one of the richest countries in the world at the beginning of last century? And then it went down the toilet. The commies trashed the country. Milei is going to make it rich again. He's incredible. He's really a great guy, very intelligent. No one has ever done what he's doing, never in the history of the world.'

'President Milei will be at your keynote, Mr President. We have a seat reserved for him in the front row.'

'And the President of Greenland? Where is the President of Greenland?' asked Donald Trump.

'Sadly, the Prime Minister of Denmark is not with us this year.'

'Shame, because I want to buy Greenland. To make America great again, we need Greenland. An absolute necessity. I'll make them an offer they can't refuse. They are going to accept it. I've never not concluded a deal and won. Ever. They'll understand, money speaks. If need be, we've got the best military in the world, the very best.'

They'd arrived in the speakers' lounge, the president's and the Don's entourages reduced to a bare minimum. On the US President side, three agents from the Secret Service, four advisers, Elon Musk and Gloria Nobow, who seemed to have emerged out of nowhere. On the Circle's side were his number two and Olena. To the Don's fury, she'd sneaked into the lounge, but it was too late to call her out and make a scandal.

'Hi, Gloria,' said the president. Great to see you: last week Mar-a-Lago, this week Davos, of all places!'

He then turned to the Don. 'Let me tell you about Gloria. She's just incredible. A tremendous friend, one of the best, believe me. She's done amazing work in the investment world, really top tier; people are saying she's the best they've seen. And she's been a great donor to my campaign. Just unbelievable support. Very religious. We love Gloria.'

He turned to her and asked, 'Is Mr Schwenk treating you well?'

Gloria Nobow glanced around the room, saw Olena. Their gazes met briefly. Both knew the other knew.

'Very well,' she replied enthusiastically. 'I'm a Davos woman by now. I'm a fan.'

'Great. This is great,' said the president, before addressing the Don, 'I hear that Russians are unfair to your participants, very unfair. Killing some here in Davos. Not good for business.'

'Well, Mr President... We don't know yet whether this is true. And I must tell you that the Graubünden cantonal police —.

Trump was not listening.

'Putin is a great guy. Can be a genius sometimes, you know? Very savvy. Strong strategic vision, like me, but he can be a bit intense, difficult. I know how to deal with him. We had a great relationship when I was the 45th president of our great nation.'

'Mr President, we have five minutes before you go on stage. It will be my great pleasure to introduce you and —'

'You should have invited Putin. We get on well. Here in Davos, we could have sorted Ukraine. Now. Just like that. Vladimir likes me. And I understand him. He has his reasons for what he does, security, geopolitical, whatever reasons. But we could make a deal. He and I would do amazing. He knows I get very high marks as a leader. Not like my predecessor, a complete, total catastrophe. One of the most overrated politicians and worst leaders America ever had. Nobody respects him but everybody respects me. Everybody knows I did an incredible job as the 45th president and will keep on doing an even more incredible job as the 47th president. I'm here to save America, the greatest country on earth. God bless America!'

Olena, a small envelop in her hand, took a step forward.

'Mr President,' she asked, handing him the envelop, 'would you mind reading this before you leave Davos?'

The Don, outraged, thought of intervening, but two Secret Service agents had already blocked the space between Olena and the president, while the third had grabbed the envelope.

'It's okay,' said Donald Trump to his bodyguards, then turned to Olena: 'You act amazing. You love being in the centre of the action. Very courageous. Like me. Do you want to take a selfie, you and me? One of my guys will put it on my social media accounts.'

'Please, Mr President, it's time,' said the Don, inviting him to the stage.

Donald Trump flashed a thumbs up, throwing a toothy lascivious grin in Olena's direction.

7 – Friday, 24 January 2025

As the glitziest event on the economic and social calendar drew to a close, the sense of excitement started to fade. The most prominent heads of state, global CEOs, finance titans, media leaders, global thinkers and change-the-world-all-at-once activists had already left. Friday would be a long descent into nothingness, when the gathering gives up its glory to entropy. No surprise there: the last day of Davos was always a dull affair, but for Olena, Dan and Phillip, it would be an entirely different story.

It was 8.00am. Taking multiple precautions to avoid a tail, all three had reached a high pasture chalet in Küblis, a 45-minute ride from Davos by car or train. Glorious in its solitude, it sat alone in a field above the small village, enjoying a breathtaking panorama. St Antönier was in the distance and, above it, the Joch pass, an ancient smugglers' route between Switzerland and Austria, sandwiched between two elegant, unassailable mountains. At Dan's pressing request, a CIA's Deputy Assistant Director General had provided the safe house at short notice. It was supposed to serve if a sensitive recruitment of a foreign asset took place during the annual meeting, but this year the US election had suspended the programme.

The safe house sat idle. Yet, the portable sensitive compartmented information facility (SCIF) that would allow them to connect with Langley and London was still in place. Five security guys from Dan's team were around, keeping a vigilant eye on the chalet and its surroundings. Another was working on resurrecting the SCIF to get it operational.

'Our call is scheduled for 9.00am,' Dan reminded them. 'Not oceans of time to figure out what the hell is going on, get our bl—dy ducks in a row and decide on next steps. Phillip, what's your assessment so far?'

'Mixed. Curate's egg – good in parts, insofar as we wanted to hit Putin where it hurts – the economy. But things have gone a bit off the rails. The initial idea to scare the s—t out of some of the crooked professionals aiding and abetting Putin's regime to evade sanctions was a good one. Giving the Russians a dose of their own medicine – creating fear and confusion – clearly works, but the "no wet work" injunction means we are operating with one hand strapped behind our backs.'

Olena was sitting beside him, but her raised eyebrows were clearly reflected on the screen in front of them both.

'*Mokroye delo* in Russian,' he filled her in. 'Eliminating or terminating someone. We don't do this. We don't kill, except in some extreme cases that require a shitload of consultation and prior authorisation.'

He went on. 'What happened to Brudov, Barbil and Clooney isn't going to be forgotten in a hurry and will serve as a clear caveat for all would-be-criminals keen to embark on the sanctions' evasion path. They'll think twice now. So far, so good – a success. But we hadn't planned on Brudov's death, nor had we bargained for the untimely overlap with the assassinations of Reginald Hubert and Caspar Munchausen. Not to mention the two bungled attempts on our lives.'

'Brudov: suicide or murder?' asked Dan.

'Murder. Almost certainly. We sent a team to the hotel. There were scratch marks on the doorknob and fragments of broken glass inside the room on the carpet. There must have a been a fight before they threw him out of the window.'

'The Russians could have read us,' suggested Olena. 'Their spooks tend to be bright. They might have seen a pattern here and decided that a compromised Brudov passed the fine line between an asset and a liability. They got rid of him.'

'Quite possible,' corroborated Dan. 'Even Caius Schwenk spotted the sanctions' thread. We might have overextended ourselves. Three was perhaps a bit greedy. One or two might have been enough.' He paused for a second before asking, 'Are we confident that Barbil and Clooney don't suspect it could be us?'

'Our guys in London are monitoring all their devices 24/7,' responded Phillip. 'So far, nothing to report. Clooney is a money-guy, a coward still digesting the shock of his life. No risk on his side. Not knowing whether it was the Russians, the mafia or someone else behind what happened, not wanting to push his luck any further, he'll hide and keep quiet. For Barbil, it's a different story. He's an old fox with connections in Russia that go back a long way. He'll try to understand what happened. He'll probably ask some questions, but before he gets to the bottom of it, which might be never, I suspect he won't talk.'

'Okay, guys, it's time. Let's connect,' said Dan. They moved back around the table, side by side, facing the camera. Dan pressed the key and the faces of one of the CIA's Deputy Assistant Directors General and a nameless senior person within the UK National Security Secretariat appeared on the screen. They were both about the same age, late 50s, but looked a decade older with dark circles around their eyes, hidden behind thick glasses, greying temples, jowly. In short: scarred by years of desk work.

As usual, the CIA ran the show, making their British counterparts look like extras. The Deputy Assistant Director General spoke first, as if it were the most natural thing in the world.

'Morning, guys. While the operation itself has been a success, some unexpected consequences could turn out to be catastrophic. To date, not much has gone exactly according to plan, and now there is a real danger of things getting majorly out of hand. My immediate concerns are twofold: first, make sure that the new US administration never, ever finds out that we exist; second, uncover what the Russians are up to. What the f—k is going on? What prompted them to eliminate Hubert, Munchausen and Brudov? How come we didn't see this coming? The contingent risks for us are considerable. Now you can be certain that everybody is at it: my American colleagues, the Swiss, the Israelis, the Chinese, the French – all trying to find out what happened in Davos. Who did what to whom.'

Dan reacted first. 'I hear what you're saying. But our only chance of getting to the bottom of this is if we can question Gloria Nobow. She's the crux – a linchpin – and as such is our best bet to crack the Russian side of this complex equation.'

'Absolutely no! You can't go anywhere near Nobow. It would be madness. She's a friend of the US President. As far as I'm concerned, it's a non-starter.'

The night before, everybody on the call had received an encrypted file prepared by the Russian desk in Langley for the Deputy Assistant Director General. It showed that Gloria Nobow, who'd been on their radar for a while, far from being a successful investor, had been struggling financially for years. Her fund had only survived thanks to Russian money. In the early 2020s, at a fundraising dinner in Washington DC, she'd met Ekaterina Brutova. Brutova was a wealthy Russian crypto-tsarina and socialite who turned her hand to using virtual currency to help Russian oligarchs launder and transfer their millions abroad. Brutova, too, had been on the CIA's radar for a while, with photos supported by recordings showing her and Nobow meeting at social events in the US, Russia and Dubai. They became friends fast, and what was destined to happen happened: Brutova offered several bridging loans to Nobow, invested in her fund and brought the odd oligarch along for the ride, a standard SVR – Russia's Foreign Intelligence Service – approach. In due course, the helping hand would turn into a kiss of death. Brutova was now under sanctions, barred from travelling to both Europe and the US but still investing in Nobow's fund through offshore entities. Shortly before Davos, she'd organised a business meeting in Istanbul at the bar of the Four Seasons at the Bosphorus, bugged by the CIA local station but the excess background noise made the recording virtually useless. Some pictures showed Brutova handing a small box to Gloria Nobow, prompting the Deputy Assistant Director General to infer that a one-sided, straightforward transaction had taken place. The conversation probably went something like this: "I won't let you down, the finance will keep coming, no questions asked, but I do need one small thing in return. When you get to Davos, at the earliest opportunity, plant this device on Olena Kostarenko. That's it, nothing more." It was a quickly sealed deal with the devil. One essential question remained: Was Gloria Nobow spying for Russia or was she just the victim of her own greed and stupidity?

Dan took matters into his own hands: 'We'll go nowhere if you don't authorize a meeting with the target. Olena can do this, softly, softly, during the Circle's farewell reception. We know Nobow's hotel reservation runs until tomorrow, so we think she'll be there.'

'Olena has already exceeded the limits of what I consider acceptable,' said the senior CIA officer, throwing her an accusatory look. 'This idea of passing an envelope to the US President is just absurd. I would never have approved it, Dan.'

'I made the decision,' replied the senator, 'and Olena is hidden behind so many layers that she'll never be associated with you or the Agency. Except for the training back in September, there is no trace of her anywhere. Only you and one of your deputies know about her current mission. If, for whatever reason, the s—t hits the fan, she'll be associated with the Brits, not with us.'

'Tough but true,' confirmed the senior British intelligence official. 'It's all been set up in such a way as to make her appear as one of us. As you know, the rental of Freedom House, the dominatrix, the "pressure" put on Barbil and Clooney, our operatives did it all. US noses are clean. That was the deal; we had the benefit of your intelligence and collaboration, but we did most of the work.'

'I still have my reservations,' insisted the senior CIA official, studiedly ignoring what his British counterpart had just said. 'If we are uncovered, if it ever emerges that we did *this*, all hell would break loose. The new president takes this sort of thing very seriously. You and I could even go to jail for sedition.'

'Come on!' said Dan. 'You know as well as I do that as soon as Gabbard is confirmed in office, you'll be unceremoniously sacked and put out to grass. The truth is, if you want to do something, it's now or never. We go with what we've got. In two- or three-weeks' time, it will be too late. We all know how extraordinarily dangerous Tulsi will be. Having her supervising our 18 intelligence agencies is like letting the fox in the henhouse. If you want to do something to stop the Russians in their tracks before it's too late, we have to act today. Don't bottle now!'

The senior official persisted. 'Taking any kind of position or action against Gloria Nobow is dynamite. It can't end well for us.'

'Who is talking about doing anything *against* her?' asked Dan. 'We just want Olena to ask her a few questions. Depending on her answers, we'll decide what to do next.'

The senior British official responded: 'I concur with my American colleague. Our government decided to embark on this black operation with you, and we are, if I may point out, the only legit part of it, but attacking or interrogating a US citizen is totally beyond our remit. As far as I'm concerned, it's a no.'

Dan's patience had run out. Exasperated, he leapt to his feet, wagging an accusatory finger at the screen. 'Get real, the two of you! Donald Trump is obsessed with the deep state, in which the intelligence community is the primary suspect. He's determined to unleash a wrecking ball aimed at all intelligence agencies and then to rebuild his own post-truth intelligence community. This will harm not only the US, but also its allies. You,' he said to his fellow American citizen, pointing his finger now trembling with rage specifically at him, 'your directorate will be the first in line – eviscerated. You and your top career officials will all be replaced by obedient political appointees. This will be the new administration's first gift to Putin. And you,' he said, shifting his ire to the British senior intelligence official, 'go figure how you'll do your job without American input. You'll be blind and deaf. Good luck! So, my point is,' concluded the senator sitting back down, 'we have to take bold and drastic action to stem the poison while there's still time. With Nobow in Davos, we have a golden opportunity.'

'Okay, I see your point,' said the CIA senior official, U-turning without so much as looking at, let alone consulting, his British peer. 'Go ahead but be careful: no violence or intimidation of any kind. I want your assurance on that.'

'Sir, what's your take?' asked Phillip to his London-based boss.

'Same here, but I'll go one step further. We don't want to get involved in this. Happy to provide unofficial physical cover and protection to Ms Kostarenko, but I'm wary of anything that might get us involved in a US-focused operation. Phillip, I don't want you, or your team, anywhere near this.'

The next 30 minutes were spent discussing the minutiae of the encounter with Gloria Nobow. All coercive options – like an intrusion into her room or a kidnapping in the street followed by an interrogation – were rejected one after the other. The CIA's Deputy Assistant Director General and the senior official from the UK National Security Secretariat only accepted the option of a "very soft" approach. Olena would find a way to engage with her target, then would strike up a conversation in which she'd ask Gloria about the origin of the microphone, and what she could tell them about her Russian handler. They'd see where this would lead and would meet again to decide about the next steps.

*****

By midday, Olena was back in Davos. She went to her flat to change for the closing reception and then straight to the funicular heading to Schatzalp. Dan had insisted she be there at least two hours in advance so two of his guys could monitor the comings and goings around the funicular and the hotel. Two more, and Paul, would ensure her safety.

Once there, she decided to take a stroll, accompanied by her three guardian angels, Paul and two Americans, discreetly deployed at an all-important distance, imperceptible to the casual onlooker but there if she needed them. She headed in the direction of Thomas-Mann-Platz, a path above the hotel, in search of a bit of perspective – metaphorical and physical – and determined to validate Friedrich Nietzsche's adage that "All truly great thoughts are conceived while walking." If ever she'd needed great, clear and creative thinking, it was now. The decision ahead of her could prove to be the most consequential she'd ever made in her short life as an intelligence operative. She needed Nietzsche's and nature's help to make the right one. The Circle farewell party would begin at 4.00pm. If Gloria Nobow happened to be there, which she thought would be the case, she had two hours to figure out how best to make contact with her.

The great peaks she'd admired from the terrace six days earlier loomed ahead of her, silent, constant and majestic, piercing the sky, like snowy daggers radiant in the early afternoon sun. She paused to take in their intemporal beauty in such a rapidly shifting world and relish the cold air on her lips, her every breath an ephemeral puff of mist that vanished into the icy brilliance. All around lay fresh snow, glistening and silent.

As she resumed her walk up the path, she let her mind wander. She knew from experience that thoughts would follow, flowing with the walk.

A flurry of images from the past few months jostled for position. She could hardly believe how fast she'd come to this point. Last April, she'd left Kyiv in haste for Washington DC where everything came together at a surprising speed. Soon after joining the think-tank, she'd befriended a fellow American researcher. He worked occasionally as a CIA talent spotter and introduced her to an official recruiter at the Agency. That's how, almost overnight, she became a valuable CIA informant, wowed by her knowledge of Ukrainian politics and of her country's relations with Russia. In a matter of weeks, she was offered the opportunity to go further and become a trusted Foreign National Officer – non-American agents doing sensitive contract work. She would never be associated with the US government in any visible way; in essence, she'd be turned into an operative who could perform clandestine operations but without any official protection or cover of any kind – one of the most dangerous positions within the Agency, apart from the Ground Branch paramilitary elite units. In September, she'd taken a tailor-made one-month crash-course to learn the basics of the "spy" trade. She'd found she loved the thrill and, except for counter-surveillance, was good at it. Now in Davos, she realised how huge the gap was between theory and practice. As the saying went, in theory, everything's always fine but, in practice, it's another kettle of fish. All one had to do to understand this chasm was to observe the calm and composure of the elite soldiers surrounding her. Throughout the week, she'd heard CEOs lecturing about their remarkable capabilities to work under pressure and make tough decisions under conditions of considerable uncertainty, but weren't these clandestine operators doing the same, only in circumstances with far greater consequences and far less room for manoeuvre? They did their training not by leafing through annual reports and swallowing notes from analysts and colleagues but by grappling with reality in its most elementary form. For these guys keeping her alive, nothing beat the book of experience.

In October things had accelerated further and then come to a head. It was at a lecture at Cornagie, a prominent think-tank, on the future of Ukraine that she met Dan Scott for the first time. During the drinks that followed, he and other veterans openly expressed their fear that a Trump administration could destroy the US by eradicating its own intelligence community, which the MAGA politicians viewed as the core of the "deep state." November and the election came, along with another series of lectures at Cornagie on Russia's and Ukraine's futures. Dan Scott and many of his peers within the intelligence community were incensed. They saw Trump's victory as a dramatic inflection point. Not only would it change their world, but it would also change the entire world, for the worst. To them, the president-elect's proposed appointments after the election looked like a decapitation strike that would destroy the American government from the top, leaving the American body politic to rot from within. Gabbard's nomination was the proverbial last straw. In the past, she'd openly embraced a world view that mirrored disinformation straight out of the Kremlin's playbook. Most intelligence veterans saw her as a Russophile who couldn't be trusted. Some argued that she might even be a Russian mole, although no evidence had ever emerged that she'd collaborated in any way with Russia's intelligence agencies. It was all simpler than that: she just shared the Kremlin's geopolitical views, especially when it came to the exercise of American military power. Within the CIA's Russian Directorate, high on the president-elect's "hate list" for its role in proving that Russia had intervened on his behalf in the 2016 elections, most agreed that she'd be Trump's armed wing, the instrument of his revenge.

At the end of November, Dan and a handful of veterans and senior intelligence officials decided to act. They'd set up a structure that would operate secretly and illegally to catch the Russians at their own game before being sacked or prevented to do so by the new administration. Over the course of many confidential meetings in Washington DC, they concocted a plan, which for necessary operational reasons involved some friendly Brits. The Circle's annual meeting in Davos would be a central part of it. Dan approached Olena. He'd made up his own mind about her. The Agency reports pointed to an inexperienced but potentially exceptional recruit. One thing leading to another, she prepared for the mission in a month. Evidently, her identity would remain secret from the outside world, but also from the CIA. And here she was, in Davos. Fear had accompanied her all the way.

These rapid reminiscences had only lasted a minute or so. She glanced at her watch: 2.30pm. She had only an hour and a half left. How best to approach Gloria? Surreptitiously? Openly? Threateningly? Aggressively? With empathy? She wasn't sure.

Ahead of her, Paul was trying to attract her attention. She moved closer and he pulled her into a clump of fir trees, out of sight.

'Miss, Phillip needs to talk to you urgently,' he said, handing her the earpiece from his two-way system. 'You can speak to him; it's encrypted, end-to-end. My mic will catch your voice,' he added, gesturing to his jacket.

She inserted the earphone into her ear. 'Yes, Phil?'

'Hi. One of our guys monitoring the messages in your Circle app just saw a message from Gloria at 2.27pm. She says the president handed to her the envelope you'd tried to give him and has asked her to meet you to discuss its content.'

'No way! Where?'

'At the Schatzalp reception. That gives us just over an hour.'

*****

Preparations proved frantic. Such operations would normally be planned weeks in advance, with every single detail being analysed, verified, double- and triple-checked. No such luxury: they had barely an hour to put everything in place and prepare for what could well be a trap. Nobody had a clue of what lay ahead.

Dan, after coordinating with his team and Phillip, went for the "all-hands-on-deck" approach. Everybody would move to Schatzalp to join Olena and the three elite soldiers already there with her. That made 14 in total: Olena plus three, Phillip and his four former SAS plus Dan and his four Ground Branch soldiers still in town. Dan and Phillip would coordinate the whole operation, but as usual the special forces would have considerable latitude to make their own decisions. They were all groomed to perform in high-risk covert operations, and the coming Schatzalp op corresponded to the kind of situation in which they excelled: volatile, uncertain, complex, ambiguous. Messy and unpredictable environments were their stock-in-trade, and they were damn good at them.

Back down in Davos, Dan convened the rest of the team in Phillip's apartment, the securest place to gather in an emergency with its garage that had been converted into a military arsenal. They had about 15 minutes to pick the weapons and equipment of their choosing and then decide together who would do what. Not knowing what to expect, they picked a variety of assault rifles, machine and submachine guns, shotguns and sidearms. The Brits chose a Glock 19 each and a combination of German-made HK416 and Heckler & Koch MG4, should the situation turn truly nasty. Apart from a Glock 19 each, including for Dan, the Americans went for their favourite Benelli M4 shotgun and a mix of FN MK48 and CZ Scorpion EVO 3 machine and submachine guns, all suppressed, with silencers built into the weapon. They decided that a sniper rifle would prove unnecessary, but one American added some flashbang grenades to his kit.

All were used to operate independently and flexibly, outside a formal hierarchy but as a team. That said, this was a scratch team with a dream-team agenda. These British and American special forces' veterans had never worked together. A minimum of coordination was therefore required and a team leader designated. By the time this was done, it was already 3.05pm.

They had no choice but to walk to Schatzalp station and take the funicular, in two teams of four and one of three. They looked a bit conspicuous in the now mostly deserted streets of Davos, but it was just possible that their overinflated backpacks could be taken for tightly packed paraglider equipment. Luckily, the Promenade had reopened. Swiss efficiency meant nothing ever took very long to go back to normal. The participants had left the Congress Centre, and the security zone had been dismantled. In just a few hours, the fences and concrete blocks would become a distant memory. The thousands of Graubünden cantonal policemen and their colleagues from other forces, together with the specially deployed 5000 military personnel, would all be gone. Soon, Davos would go back to being just a quiet little mountain town nestling in the Albula Alps.

Meanwhile, up in Schatzalp, Paul had organised an emergency briefing with Olena and his two American bros deep in the woods. There was no time to do better than that. He was in constant contact with Phillip, passing the information to Olena in real time. He explained to her in detail how they intended to conduct the whole operation, how they'd protect her, and conveyed Dan and Phillips' decision to leave it up to her to choose for herself when and where to connect with Gloria Nobow. All 14 would be equipped with the same encrypted two-way communication system. It meant they had to be sparing with words and disciplined. All 14 could hear, but only one person at a time could speak. The ultra-powerful, quasi-invisible, micro-mic made it possible to do so naturally, but discretion was still required to avoid arousing curiosity. Only in the case of a major problem would they warn Olena to break and abandon. Otherwise, she was to proceed as she saw fit.

Since nobody knew whether Gloria's request to meet was genuine or not, or if a Russian ambush was a possibility, although unorthodox, this seemed to be the most sensible path.

It was now 3.45pm. The first guests had begun to arrive, groups of white badges being spewed at regular intervals from the carriages of the blue and yellow funicular. The entirely coincidental but serendipitous colourway had not gone unnoticed by Olena. Good or bad omen – who knew! Out of the 3000 white badges who'd come to Davos that week, the Circle was only expecting about 300 to attend that afternoon's reception. The end was nigh, their guard was down and, for the first time in five days, there'd be no badge scan and no X-ray machine, only eye-control from Securitas' agents and the occasional bag inspection. For Phillip and the rest of the team, the counterfeit white badges prepared in London by the tech team would do the trick.

One of Dan's guys had been posted at the Panorama restaurant, just above the funicular's arrival, to spot the presence of Gloria Nobow or any suspicious activity and possible tail. The others were arranging themselves as agreed, between the funicular and the Hotel Schatzalp, 100 metres away, and in the hotel's Belle Epoque and Snow Beach restaurants, where the reception had just started. Olena was nervously waiting in the crowd, vaguely smiling at people she knew. Paul hovered close by, giving nothing away. Four other team members had spread out to the four corners of the room, plus two at each end of the Snow Beach's terrace. The atmosphere was friendly, relaxed, with the Don greeting his guests with a palpable air of self-satisfaction – contentment even.

By his own metric – the number of super V-VIPs in attendance – this year's Davos had been a success, sidelining the scandals that had marred the meeting and upstaging the paucity of new ideas. The self-congratulatory mood was contagious.

While scanning the room and assiduously avoiding bumping into the Don, Olena heard in her earpiece a team member warning that Gloria was on her way, seemingly alone. She spotted her on the terrace, coming into the Belle Epoque. True to form, she was ebullient, confident, determined and as glamorous in the mountains as she was in the city. Heads turned. She was wearing a silver Palm Angels Moncler jacket with matching trousers, out glistening the snow beyond. If she'd wanted to go unnoticed, she hadn't. She headed straight to Olena, at the other end of the restaurant, as if she were the only person there.

'Hi, darling, so very nice to see you!'

'Likewise,' stammered Olena, a little disconcerted.

'You and I have a lot to talk about. The president loved your letter.'

'Did he? Great.'

'Give me a minute,' said Gloria. 'I just need to go to the restroom. I'll be right back. Why don't you wait for me outside? No! On second thought, let's take a stroll; it'll be quieter and more invigorating! Why don't we walk towards this famous Thomas-Mann-Platz that everybody talks about. Apparently, it's not far. I'll see you there!'

'Okay. Yes... see you... there,' complied Olena, after a moment of hesitation.

Gloria disappeared. Olena moved to the terrace, half-a-dozen special ops regrouping around her. Paul seemed to be coordinating their manoeuvres using quasi-imperceptible eye movements. She heard Dan instructing the former Ground Branch woman to follow Gloria to the ladies' restroom. 'No contact, Sabina. Just keep an eye at a distance.'

Now out of anyone else's earshot, Olena asked, mild panic in her voice, 'Where's "there?" I don't under—'

Then Sabina's voice broke in. 'She's gone. Unless there is another ladies' room, she's vanished.'

Two former Ground Branch quickly circled the hotel in opposite directions and returned empty-handed.

'What the f—k is going on?' asked Dan. 'Where is she? Matt and Tom, check the other restaurants now. Noah and Henry, widen the scope – the funicular, the paths above and below. The rest of us, wait here with Olena.'

Noah and Henry had reached the far side of the building. One of them suddenly said, 'Spotted, she's outside already walking in the direction of Thomas-Mann-Platz.

There's a woman with her. And a couple, man and woman, just ahead of her.'

'How far ahead?' asked Dan.

'100-150 metres.'

'Badge holders?'

'Can't be sure but dressed as if coming from the reception. No sign of coercion.'

'Facial clues?'

'Negative, but a bit too far to be 100 per cent.'

'We won't have another chance,' Olena said. 'Let's follow her.'

'I don't like the look of this,' interjected Phillip. 'It smells like a trap to me.'

Dan insisted. 'Olena is right. It's now or never. It could well be a trap, but it's not certain. She might just have come across a participant she knew. We have 11 top special ops with us. I'm ready to take the risk.'

The whole group moved away from the crowd, standing in front of the terrace. Dan and Phillip left it to the special ops to decide how best to proceed.

Three guys would scout the path and its surroundings, sweeping it and making sure Gloria was clean notwithstanding her current companions. The rest of the group would follow 50 metres behind. The ever-present risk of a sniper meant that four special ops would form a shell around Olena in between the hotel and the forest, 200 metres away. The time for discretion had passed. Establishing contact with Gloria was the only thing that mattered, and they were counting on the farewell party, now in full swing, to provide the cover they needed.

For the first few minutes, things went off without a hitch. The scouting team was progressing well, although Gloria had slipped out of sight.

Olena, Dan, Phillip and the rest of the team were following, their boots crunching on the frozen snow crust, barely breaking the silence. Gloria was still nowhere to be seen. An unspeakable feeling of unease was mounting, their collective sixth sense signalling red alert.

Suddenly, one of the scouts hissed in their ear: 'Blood stains in the snow, every two metres or so on the path. Diagonal tracks heading into the forest. Four I think. More blood.'

Olena, Dan, Phillip and Paul took cover under the branches of a big fir tree, two of the British operatives covering their backs from a few metres away. All the others continued to follow the trail of dripping blood, focused only on the asset, deployed in the forest, spaced out from one another, casting a wide, methodical net, their weapons at the ready hand, in pursuit, predatory.

'Confirmed,' said one. 'Four different tracks, heading straight into the forest.'

'What the f—k is Gloria up to?' said Dan. 'You can be certain it's no walk in the park.'

Hidden by the branches of the fir tree, they could do nothing but follow the progression of the team in their earpiece.

No unnecessary words were heard, only the occasional 'No movement at 9 o'clock,' 'clear ahead,' 'regroup,' and the like.

Suddenly, one said, 'Target at 12 o'clock, lying in the snow, soaked in blood. I'm making contact.' Then, 'It's Nobow. Dead. One bullet in the forehead and one in the heart.'

'Regroup on the path,' instructed Dan.

The next thing they heard was the sound of a gunshot in the distance. For a few seconds all was quiet, until the staccato of a submachine gun resonated through the forest, muffled by the silencer.

A long silence followed, broken by the occasional interjections of the special ops, when, unexpectedly, a bullet whizzed by the fir tree. Someone was shooting just a few metres away. Olena screamed. Paul threw himself over her. Another bullet splintered a branch just above them in a narrow miss. Voices and shouts rose from beyond the path, mixing with those crackling from the two-way communication system and the rat-tat-tat of submachine guns overpowering the crack of the handguns.

When Olena lifted her head, just a few seconds later, it was all over. Calm had reclaimed the mountains.

The special op who'd discovered the body of Gloria handed Dan a note. 'It was on her chest,' he said.

The note read: "Lieutenant General Igor Kirillov, Head of Russia's Radiation, Chemical and Biological Defence Forces. In Memoriam."

*****

The last guests had gone, leaving Schatzalp deserted. The three of them, lost in their own thoughts, were on the terrace, Olena on the very same wicker lounger where she'd sat six days earlier. The special ops were roaming around, the secret world reeling from collateral damage. Gloria Nobow was the latest casualty.

'Hubert and Munchausen and now Gloria look like the Kremlin's revenge for Kirillov's assassination,' said Dan. 'Ever since his killing in Moscow a month ago, the Russians have been claiming that the Ukrainians couldn't have done it without the US. Putin's paranoia playing out. And an unequivocal welcome message to the new incumbent of the White House. "Bros maybe – but on whose terms?"'

'Just how involved was the CIA?' asked Phillip.

Dan was immersed in the contemplation of the mountains. 'What do I know?' he muttered, still absorbed by the chiselled peaks of the Strela and Wannagrat, incandescent in the setting sunshine. 'I left the Agency too long ago. The thing about intelligence is, if it's known, it ceases to be intelligence. Could be. Maybe we are just "squabbling" over red lines.'

'We are all just trying to do the best we can,' said Phillip, 'and more often than not failing miserably. The spooks are the only realists left in the world. I think it was le Carré who said it. Too many of the Davos crowd choose to ignore reality even when it happens inside their very own "snow globe" - they have no idea. Le Carré was right.'

He then turned to Olena. 'There are two things I've been wanting to ask you.'

'What, Phil?'

'At your flat, the hair on the door frame, was it for real?'

'You're not a bad spook after all! Or perhaps you know me better than I thought you did,' she exclaimed with a laugh. 'No, it was not. I was just terrified and couldn't imagine staying on my own. Question number two?'

'The Don? What did you tell him to get a white badge so easily?'

'That's my own little secret. Let's just say I made him an offer that he couldn't refuse.'

Printed in Great Britain
by Amazon